"The Object Lessons series achieves something very close to magic: the books take ordinary—even banal—objects and animate them with a rich history of invention, political struggle, science, and popular mythology. Filled with fascinating details and conveyed in sharp, accessible prose, the books make the everyday world come to life. Be warned: once you've read a few of these, you'll start walking around your house, picking up random objects, and musing aloud: 'I wonder what the story is behind this thing?'"

Steven Johnson, author of *Where Good Ideas Come From* and *How We Got to Now*

"Object Lessons describes themselves as 'short, beautiful books,' and to that, I'll say, amen. . . . If you read enough Object Lessons books, you'll fill your head with plenty of trivia to amaze and annoy your friends and loved ones—caution recommended on pontificating on the objects surrounding you. More importantly, though . . . they inspire us to take a second look at parts of the everyday that we've taken for granted. These are not so much lessons about the objects themselves, but opportunities for self-reflection and storytelling. They remind us that we are surrounded by a wondrous world, as long as we care to look.'"

John Warner, *The Chicago Tribune*

OBJECT LESSONS

A book series about the hidden lives of ordinary things.

Series Editors:

Ian Bogost and Christopher Schaberg

Advisory Board:

Sara Ahmed, Jane Bennett, Jeffrey Jerome Cohen,
Johanna Drucker, Raiford Guins, Graham Harman,
renée hoogland, Pam Houston, Eileen Joy, Douglas
Kahn, Daniel Miller, Esther Milne, Timothy Morton,
Kathleen Stewart, Nigel Thrift, Rob Walker, Michele White.

In association with

BOOKS IN THE SERIES

souvenir

ROLF POTTS

BLOOMSBURY ACADEMIC
NEW YORK · LONDON · OXFORD · NEW DELHI · SYDNEY

197533

306
4819
POT

BLOOMSBURY ACADEMIC
Bloomsbury Publishing Inc
1385 Broadway, New York, NY 10018, USA

BLOOMSBURY, BLOOMSBURY ACADEMIC and the Diana logo
are trademarks of Bloomsbury Publishing Plc

First published in the United States of America 2018

Cover design: Alice Marwick

A catalog record for this book is available from the Library of Congress.

ISBN: PB: 978-1-5013-2941-8
ePDF: 978-1-5013-2942-5
eBook: 978-1-5013-2944-9

Series: Object Lessons

Typeset by Deanta Global Publishing Services, Chennai, India
Printed and bound in the United States of America

To find out more about our authors and books visit www.bloomsbury.com
and sign up for our newsletters.

We collect to survive; our survival depends in part on our ability to classify and codify and catalogue: we hunt and choose in order to tame chaos, to bring order to a world too full of being, too full of things. . . . Over our possessions, we allow ourselves to believe, we have control. With our possessions we weave our shrouds. Everything we collect is a memento mori.

—Barbara Grizzuti Harrison, *An Accidental Autobiography* (1997)

CONTENTS

Mongolian Tsaghan Ebügen mask,
author's collection, 2001

PREFACE

I t has been a recurring daydream for me, as I've written this book, that it will one day be stocked in gift-shop stalls around the world, from the British Museum in London, to Disneyland in Anaheim, to Bangkok's Chatuchak Market. That way, should the breadth of souvenir options on offer overwhelm a given tourist, he or she can simply go meta and commemorate the travel experience with this book, *Souvenir*.

In a way, this is a souvenir guidebook of sorts—not a rundown of what items to collect, or where to find them, but an exploration of why we seek out these objects as we travel, what they have represented to travelers in past ages, and how we use them to narrate our lives.

My earliest memory of collecting souvenirs goes back to age seven, when I took a series of Amtrak trains to Chicago with my family. It was the furthest I'd ever traveled from my South Central Kansas home, and the giant Midwestern metropolis full of skyscrapers, museums, and traffic jams struck me as wonderfully exotic. I was particularly enamored with the ocean-like expanse of Lake Michigan, and one afternoon, while walking along a pebbled lakeside beach, I happened upon a large white clamshell ribbed with brownish-yellow stripes. Thrilled at this discovery, I squirreled the clamshell away in my knapsack, and it eventually found a place of honor in my bedroom. Over time, this shell became the centerpiece of a makeshift shrine that held other travel souvenirs—pins, coins, pebbles, embroidered patches, figurines, ticket stubs.

As I grew older I added to this piecemeal souvenir collection without thinking much about why I had been drawn to the items in question. Sometimes my travel souvenirs were found objects; other times these objects had been purchased from vendors or given to me as gifts. It wasn't until I moved to Asia to work as an English teacher in my mid-twenties that I realized how each of these souvenirs hinted at narratives that were far more complex—far more connected to my core sense of self—than I'd previously assumed.

My moment of epiphany came in the summer of 2001, when, having just purchased a small shamanistic mask in Ulan Bator, I realized I had no idea why I'd felt compelled to buy it. The mask in question—a yellow-painted visage of a long-bearded old man (known as *Tsaghan Ebügen* in Mongolian)—was the sixth ceremonial mask I'd purchased in as many countries since arriving in Asia five years earlier. In China, I'd bought an ornate white opera mask; in Japan, I'd bought a demonic-looking red mask used in *Gigaku* dance drama; in Korea, I'd bought a black *Nojang* mask used in satirical *talchum* plays.

As it happened, I had not attended (nor developed a particular interest in) any *talchum* plays, *Gigaku* dance drama, or Chinese operas. Furthermore, I later discovered that the red-green monster mask I'd acquired in Thailand had been manufactured in Bali, and the moon-shaped ebony mask I'd bought in the Philippines bore more similarities to Mexican flea-market craft than Filipino art traditions. None of the masks were big enough to cover a person's face, and I'd acquired them not at cultural events but at gift shops, outdoor markets, and (in the case of the Chinese opera mask) a massive department store.

Had my souvenir-collecting ritual devolved into a superficial consumer ritual that had little to do with the cultures I was visiting? By a certain superficial way of looking at it: yes, I'd reckon it had. But the more I thought about it, the more I realized that few of the souvenirs I'd collected over the course of my life had been straightforward signifiers of a specific place, culture, or personal experience. Even the clamshell I'd plucked from the shore of Lake Michigan all those years earlier had never purely been about remembering Chicago. Though as an adult I recognized it as a freshwater mollusk carapace, I'd spent most of my childhood calling it a "seashell." As it happened, this found clamshell wasn't just a memento of the wonder I'd felt at seeing Lake Michigan; it was—for me, as a kid—a totem of faith that I might one day travel beyond the landlocked prairies of my youth, see an actual ocean, collect a real seashell, and journey outward to farther shores.

Similarly, my compulsion to collect ceremonial masks while I wandered Asia was tied to something deeper and more aspirational: something that would continue to transform for me over time, and come to resonate in ways I can still sense today; something universal, even as it felt personal; something interwoven with the way we all try to make sense of the world, and our place in it.

This subtle mystery—this aura—underpinning souvenirs (and the ways we collect them) is a phenomenon I will explore in depth as this book travels through four millennia of human history before finding its way back to that moment in Mongolia, and everything it might have represented.

Eiffel Tower keychains, Par'ici display rack, 2016

1 INTRODUCTION: AN EMBARRASSMENT OF EIFFEL TOWERS

At Par'ici, a souvenir shop located at 52 Rue Mouffetard in Paris, almost every item on offer has something to do with the Eiffel Tower. Here, in 270 square feet of cramped showroom space, with Charles Trénet and Édith Piaf tunes warbling in the background, one can buy Eiffel Tower T-shirts and Eiffel Tower snow globes; Eiffel Tower whiskey flasks and Eiffel Tower oven mitts; Eiffel Tower bottle openers and Eiffel Tower ashtrays. The music boxes here come with Eiffel Towers engraved on the outside; berets come with Eiffel Towers silhouetted in sequins.

For unexpected weather, Par'ici sells Eiffel Tower-themed umbrellas, sun hats, and scarves; for amusement, it sells Eiffel Tower-embossed soccer balls, poker chips, and Rubik's Cubes. Several dozen types of Eiffel Tower miniatures are also on offer, from inch-high plastic key chains that cost 0.50 euros, to bronze lawn ornaments that stand four-and-a-half-feet tall and sell for 890 euros each. The store also offers a fair selection of items that don't allude to the Eiffel Tower (Mona Lisa shot glasses, plastic cancan-dancer figurines, ballpoint pens in the shape of baguettes, etc.), but for the most part Eiffel Tower products dominate.

A central irony here is that 52 Rue Mouffetard is not particularly close to the Eiffel Tower. One cannot glimpse the Tower from any point along this cobblestoned thoroughfare, and a pedestrian would need to walk west for one hour to reach the monument on foot. It is because of this seeming anomaly—not in spite of it—that Par'ici feels like a fitting place to begin our investigation of souvenirs.

In French, the word *souvenir* is commonly used as a verb, and means "to get back to myself," or "to remember" (from the Latin *subvenire*, "to come to mind"). In English "souvenir" is a noun—an object through which something (a place, a person, an experience) is remembered. This English definition dates back to the 1700s, though it didn't come into widespread use until the late nineteenth century—about the same time mass-market travel gift shops first began to pop up in places like Paris.

I've been teaching creative writing at the Paris American Academy each summer since 2002, and I often pass by Par'ici on my way to or from school. Rue Mouffetard, an Ernest Hemingway haunt back in the 1920s, is a lively pedestrian street full of atmospheric restaurants and cafés. Though popular with tourists during the summer months, Rue Mouffetard is not, by Paris standards, a major tourist area.

Nonetheless, Par'ici is one of two shops plying the souvenir trade along this short thoroughfare. Its competitor, Obj'Ai Trouvé, located just seven storefronts away, also features an abundance of Eiffel Tower-themed trinkets.

Both of these stores sit in the heart of the city's Fifth Arrondissement, a one-square-mile Left Bank district that, at the time of this writing, is home to thirty-three distinct tourist-market gift shops (with names like Au Chic Souvenir, Paris Smile Souvenirs, Paris Star Souvenirs, Rose for You, and Gift Paradise). More than a dozen Fifth Arrondissement newsstands also sell tourist knickknacks, as do museum shops in the Jardin des Plantes and the Musée national du Moyen Âge. Add in the souvenir items on offer at the various antique stores, bookshops, jewelry boutiques, and art galleries—as well as the green-box *bouquinistes* vendor-stalls along the Seine—and one can scarcely walk three blocks in the Fifth Arrondissement without being presented with dozens of souvenir-buying options.

This is all more remarkable for the fact that the Fifth Arrondissement isn't among the top five tourist districts in Paris—not when compared to the First (home to the Louvre and the Tuileries), the Fourth (the Notre Dame and the Pompidou), the Eighth (the Champs-Élysées and the Arc de Triomphe), or even the Eighteenth (Montmartre and Sacré-Cœur). The Seventh Arrondissement features the Eiffel Tower itself, which attracts so many souvenir vendors that a 2011 attempt to evict unlicensed salespeople from the area required a deployment of riot-control police (three of whom were injured when the besieged tchotchke-peddlers began hurling rocks and bottles). The following spring French customs police busted the street vendors' Paris-based ringleaders, seizing 13 tons of unlicensed miniature Eiffel Towers in the process.

When I first learned of this—13 *tons* of contraband Eiffel Tower kitsch!—I found it hard to believe that Par'ici, a shop three miles away, in a much quieter part of the city, could stay in business. Eventually curiosity got the best of me, and I introduced myself to the store's 59-year-old owner, Désirée Taieb, who runs Par'ici with her son Sebastian. Her shop, she told me, dates back to 1992, and she set it up with the help of her sister, who peddles similar merchandise just up the block at Obj'Ai Trouvé. Désirée has, in the past, dabbled in more traditional fare (such as handmade porcelain dolls in French peasant costumes), but ultimately tourists are more inclined to buy mass-produced *bijouterie*. "We sell Eiffel Tower things," she told me, "because people want Eiffel Tower things."

*

While Paris is one of the most heavily touristed cities in the world, the market for travel souvenirs has also seeped into the planet's most desolate and remote corners—a fact I was reminded of during a recent journey to Namibia's Skeleton Coast in southwestern Africa. This desert-parched, rock-strewn stretch of Atlantic coastline south of the Angolan border has an end-of-the-earth feel; sixteenth-century

Portuguese sailors called it "The Gates of Hell," while Namibian Bushmen called it "The Land God Made in Anger." Apart from a smattering of picturesque sand dunes and scientific research outposts, the only tourist draws here are the bleached whalebones and rotting shipwrecks that litter the coastline. Still, it is difficult to drive the length of the Skeleton Coast without spotting a few Damara tribesmen selling polished rocks along the roadside.

By African souvenir standards, polished rocks are something of a novelty. Visit any tourist-town craft bazaar in southern Africa—in the Namibian coastal resort of Swakopmund, for example, or in Cape Town's sprawling Pan-African Market—and the offerings are consistent to the point of being standardized. Much like Parisian gift shops focus on Eiffel Towers and Mona Lisas, African souvenir-market stalls carry some combination of hardwood serving bowls, safari-animal figurines, tribal-ceremony masks, beaded bracelets, engraved ostrich eggs, warthog-tusk bottle openers, and hand-dyed batiks. Ask African market-vendors why these particular items are on sale, and you'll get an answer similar to the one I got in Paris: years of trial and error have shown that these objects—which evoke a romanticized, if faintly generic, vision of the African continent—are what tourists want.

Curiously enough, market demand is also what has drawn Damara rock vendors to the forlorn highways of the Skeleton Coast. Historically, the Damara were among the original inhabitants of what has now become Namibia, and their Khoekhoe language features clicking sounds distinctive to the region. The arrival of powerful Bantu-speaking tribes (and, later, German colonialists) in the nineteenth century pushed the Damara out of their traditional hunting and grazing regions and into a desolate, mountainous area in the northwestern part of the country. Though water was scarce in this part of Namibia, the mountains yielded semiprecious stones—turquoise, amethyst, garnets, tiger's eye, tourmaline—that were prized by German and Afrikaans settlers. The stone trade proved so profitable that the Damara, who had typically lived as subsistence pastoralists, began to travel out of the mountains to sell rocks along Namibia's major roadways. As the country's tourist infrastructure grew over the course of the twentieth century, the roadside rock trade grew with it.

I learned all of this from Johannes !Hara-|Nurob, a 41-year-old Damara elder who hawks semiprecious stones on a beach near the *Zeila* shipwreck, thirty-five miles north of Swakopmund. Though Johannes plies his trade more than seven thousand miles away from Paris, his no-nonsense pragmatism reminded me of Désirée Taieb and Par'ici. Shipwrecks are major tourist attractions along the Skeleton Coast, so when the *Zeila* (an Angolan fishing boat) ran aground here in 2008, Johannes was one of a dozen Damara vendors who turned up to sell rocks to sightseers. The Damara work the beach in teams of three, taking turns as each new tourist car arrives; on a good day, a three-man team can split $50 worth of sales—though it's not uncommon to sell no stones at all when tourist traffic is light. Johannes and his colleagues live on the beach near the *Zeila* full-time between November and February, returning in the off-season to their home villages, where they spend time with their families, raise cattle, and dig for more rocks up in the mountains.

When I asked Johannes what traditional Damara life was like before the stone trade, he told me that he wasn't sure—that, for him, Damara tribal identity is inseparable from selling souvenirs. "For as long as white people have been coming to Namibia we have been selling them rocks," he said. "My father sold rocks, and my grandfather too; I grew up doing the same. To me, this *is* traditional Damara life."

*

I should probably point out that the very definition of what constitutes a souvenir can be a slippery concept. Some people who buy, say, a chunk of rose quartz from Johannes on the Skeleton Coast might display it back home as a reminder of Namibia; others might resell it at a profit without taking much interest in what it represents at a personal level. On that same token, many people collect non-travel objects—mementos, keepsakes, heirlooms, trophies, antiques, memorabilia—that have souvenir-like qualities while not being souvenirs in the literal sense. In the interest of simplicity, I'm going to focus on objects that are collected for personal reasons during the course of a journey.

Academic researchers have pinpointed five different categories of souvenirs that people seek out in their travels. The stones sold by Johannes and other Damara vendors in Namibia are considered "piece-of-the-rock"—physical fragments of the travel destination or experience itself. This time-honored souvenir category encompasses everything from pebbles and seashells, to ticket stubs and emptied wine bottles. Usually this type of souvenir is found or kept at no extra cost, though (as is the case with Namibian turquoise, Latvian amber, or chunks of the Berlin Wall) it is sometimes collected and sold by enterprising vendors. A second souvenir category, "local products," includes everything from Uruguayan leatherwork, to Mozambican *piri-piri* sauce, to the Parisian fashion designs found in the boutiques along Rue Mouffetard.

While these first two souvenir types predate the tourism industry, the final three souvenir categories encompass the mass-market objects one finds in places like Par'ici: "pictorial images," which includes postcards and posters depicting local iconography and attractions; "markers," which includes T-shirts, coffee mugs, and other products branded to the location; and "symbolic shorthand," which includes miniaturized Eiffel Towers and Notre Dames. Since these three types of souvenirs can be manufactured in bulk and shipped most anywhere within the globalized economy, they tend to represent just how abstracted the relationship between souvenir and place has become in the twenty-first century.

In Par'ici, for example, Désirée has set out small signs indicating specific items that were made in France—but this only underscores the fact that a majority of the souvenirs sold here (and indeed in most Paris gift shops) were manufactured in distant Chinese factories. Moreover, thanks to Désirée's tech-savvy son Sebastian, one need not even visit Paris to purchase these souvenirs, since the Par'ici website, souvenirparis.com, features an online store that includes international shipping, a blog with virtual tours of the city, and a link to the store's Instagram account (@souvenirparis, which boasts more than 10,000 followers from around the world).

When one ponders the prospect of going online and ordering a Guangzhou-made miniature Eiffel Tower and having it shipped from Paris to Dubuque without the need to set foot in France, it is tempting to write off the souvenir ritual as an exercise in postmodern absurdity. Yet, while each Eiffel Tower tchotchke displayed on the shelves of Par'ici enters the store with generic commercial value, it exits the store as part of an individualized narrative (even when Sebastian wraps it up and mails it to a place like Iowa). Like all souvenirs, the object's personal meaning gains potency as it moves away from the place that imbues it with objective meaning.

In a sense, souvenirs are a metaphor for how lived experience can endow most any object with personal significance. To understand how even mass-produced kitsch can become rich with meaning to the traveler who collects it, we must first hearken back to the earliest recorded journeys, when travel was difficult, and the objects one collected on a journey were considered sacred.

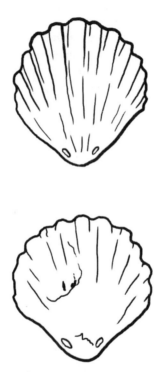

Santiago de Compostela pilgrim badge, 15th century

2 SOUVENIRS IN THE AGE OF PILGRIMAGE

As Christian pilgrimage to the Holy Land became fashionable in the centuries following the Crucifixion, pilgrims' enthusiasm for sacred souvenirs began to create problems for the custodians of Jerusalem's shrines. On the Mount of Olives, for example, the main pilgrim attraction was the Sanctuary of the Ascension, built to commemorate the Gospel account of Christ's final moments on earth before departing into heaven. To underscore the drama of this miraculous moment, a portion of the sanctuary floor had been left unpaved, and tradition asserted that the footprints of Jesus could still be discerned in the exposed dirt. Eager to possess a bit of the dust that had touched the messiah's feet, visiting pilgrims began to spirit away fistfuls of the sanctuary floor in such profusion that the shrine's caretakers were forced to haul in fresh dirt every few weeks.

In some ways modern tourism in the West traces back to the Christian rite of pilgrimage, which was the primary form of personally motivated, nonmilitary, noncommercial travel in the Middle Ages. Granted, some core aspects of pilgrimage (the months of walking, the constant fear of illness and death) don't factor much in a modern jet vacation—but there is a sense in which both experiences serve to validate the existence of a distant, once-imagined reality. In this sense, buying an Eiffel Tower key chain in Paris carries faint echoes of the pilgrim's impulse to pilfer dirt from the Sanctuary of the Ascension. "People feel the need to bring things home with them from the sacred, extraordinary time or space, for home is equated with ordinary, mundane time and space," scholar Beverly Gordon observed. "They can't hold on to the non-ordinary experience, for it is by nature ephemeral, but they can hold on to a tangible piece of it, an object that came from it."

No doubt the impulse to make faraway places tangible by collecting objects predates recorded history. One imagines an ancient hunter collecting shimmering stones from a distant mountain to share with his children back home, or an ancient gatherer bringing her husband exotic flowers from a berry-picking excursion in an unfamiliar valley. The earliest tribal religions attributed supernatural powers to objects, and oftentimes these devotional "fetishes" were in essence travel souvenirs—items that were imbued with an aura of magic by dint of their larger-than-life foreignness.

Some of the earliest recorded travel-souvenir objects were gifts brought home from cross-cultural journeys. When

Prince Harkhuf of Egypt traveled to Sudan around 2200BC, for example, he collected leopard skins, elephant tusks, ebony, and incense to present to the pharaoh. A few centuries later, in ancient Mesopotamia, gifts had become so central to the travel ritual that an 1800BC letter from a certain Adad-abum to his father Uzalum is ripe with presumption. "Get me a fine string full of beads, to be worn around the head," he writes as his father embarks on a diplomatic trip from Ashnunna (north of modern-day Baghdad) to a subject city known for its jewelry. "I want it very much; do not withhold it from me. In this I will see whether you love me as a real father does!"

By the time of the ancient Greeks and Romans, manufactured souvenirs had become a cottage industry around religious and recreational sites. Visitors to Alexandria in the second century BC could buy inexpensive faience pots engraved with images of Ptolemaic queens, while travelers to the tombs of Achilles and Patroklos in Troy could buy silver miniatures of area temples. Antioch, famous for its giant statue of Tyche, did a steady trade in small glass bottles resembling the goddess of luck, while the artists of Athens painted on-the-spot souvenir portraits of travelers posing in front of sights like the Parthenon. Well-to-do Roman ancients visiting the coastal resort of Baiae could buy little glass vials etched with pictures of such local attractions as the lighthouse, the oyster beds, and Nero's Pool, while the satirist Lucian wrote sardonically of the kitschy pottery and cheap statuettes sold near the famed statue of Aphrodite at Knidos.

The recurrence of mythic and religious imagery here is significant, since shrines proved to be the most reliable souvenir economy in the ancient world. This wasn't a phenomenon confined to the Mediterranean, either: In India, Hindu pilgrims visiting the Shiva temples of Varanasi often bought glass phalluses (*linga*) to commemorate the visit, while Buddhist visitors to Bodhgaya could choose between miniature dried-clay stupas, stone steles depicting events from Buddha's life, or small models of Mahabodhi temple. One of the most iconic souvenir rituals of the Muslim hajj to Mecca—buying an ornate container to collect water from the sacred spring of Zamzam—predates the emergence Islam, and resembles similar pilgrim rituals dating back to the ancient shrines of the god Isis on the banks of the Egyptian Nile.

The most colorful, far-reaching, and well-documented travel rite from ancient history is the tradition of Christian pilgrimage, which emerged in earnest around the fourth century AD, and thrived in various parts of Europe and the Holy Land for more than a millennium. Within this Christian tradition (which had deep pagan roots), objects collected as souvenirs of one person's pilgrimage often became relics in and of themselves, begetting new shrines and souvenirs for subsequent generations of pilgrims.

The earliest Christian pilgrimages focused on Jerusalem, where pilgrims sought to follow the footsteps of Jesus, beholding the sites of his birth, ministry, miracles, and Crucifixion. On a psychic level the long, difficult journey to the Holy Land was an act of penance and hard-won thanksgiving; at a spiritual level, it was meant to symbolize the journey of one's own existence, from birth, through an ongoing progression of earthly tribulations, to the end goal, which was heavenly salvation. Life, it was thought, was itself a pilgrimage.

Though seeking Jerusalem as a holy destination was a metaphor for faith in action, the pilgrims who arrived there tended to seek out concrete proof of divine events. The most popular shrines featured high-profile objects from the life of Christ, such as the crown of thorns, the cup used at the Last Supper, and the True Cross. In "A Short Description of Jerusalem," written by an anonymous pilgrim around AD 500, the rundown of relics on display in the holy city strains the credulity of the modern reader, listing such items as "the horn with which David and Solomon were anointed," "the stone with which Stephen was stoned," and "the earth of which Adam was formed."

As was the case with the soil taken from the Sanctuary of the Ascension, pilgrims liked to collect tangible evidence of their divine destination. Some souvenirs harvested by the pilgrims—wax drippings from sanctuary candles, charcoal rubbings of shrine inscriptions, flasks of water from the Jordan River—posed little problem to the custodians of sacred sites. Often, however, religious travelers enamored of holy relics could prove obnoxious. In one notorious instance, a pilgrim who'd been allowed to kiss the True Cross on Good Friday managed to chew off a sizeable splinter of wood and steal away with it in his mouth. Eventually, Jerusalem's ecclesiastical tour-guides took it upon themselves to lecture newly arrived pilgrims on the protocols of how to behave in the city; high on the list of verboten activities was carving graffiti onto sacred monuments, or hammering off chunks as keepsakes.

In a certain modern-minded sense, sacred souvenirs gave pilgrims a tangible token of their faith, and an object through which to remember their ephemeral experience of the holy city. To the pilgrims of the Middle Ages, however, the items they brought home from Jerusalem were also considered magic talismans capable of performing miracles. This belief in the supernatural power of objects has its roots in the fetish-rites of prehistory, but medieval Christians took their cues from Acts 19:11–12, which asserts that "God did extraordinary miracles through Paul, so that even handkerchiefs and aprons that had touched him were taken to the sick, and their illnesses were cured and the evil spirits left them."

Citing the example of Saint Paul (and, no doubt, hoping to preempt theft and vandalism at shrines), pilgrims in Jerusalem were encouraged to buy clay tablets, strips of cloth, or jars of water, which—after having been rubbed up against relics, shrines, or the bones of saints—were taken home as sacred charms. This belief in "contact relics" was so widely held that when the Dominican friar Felix Fabri departed for the Holy Land in 1483, he packed a bag of jewels that could be pressed against relics and distributed to friends and patrons when he got home.

As had been the case at ancient Greek and Roman pilgrimage sites, Jerusalem also developed a market in manufactured souvenirs. Since holy oil from the city's shrines and tombs was a prized keepsake, embossed flasks known as *ampullae* proved to be a hot commodity. The most common such container—a small, hexagonal glass bottle decorated with crosses—was produced by local artisans, but market stalls also featured religious-themed handicrafts imported from distant cities (including cheap terra-cotta jugs that were purchased in bulk from Alexandria and painted to suit the various shrines). Pilgrims not interested in *ampullae* could commemorate their Jerusalem sojourn by purchasing crucifixes, engraved medallions, silver bells, wooden miniatures of holy places, and small paintings of biblical scenes.

The most iconic souvenir of a Holy Land pilgrimage was the Palm of Jericho (two crossed palm fronds), which, pinned to the clothing as a badge, symbolized the resurrection of Christ and the victory of faith over sin. At first it was customary for pilgrims to journey twenty miles out of Jerusalem and collect palms from the plain along the Jordan River—a ritual that William of Tyre, writing in 1180, called "the formal sign that the pilgrim's vow has been fulfilled." By the thirteenth century, however, enterprising merchants harvested palm fronds en masse from the river-plain, hauled them to Jerusalem, and sold them in the city's Rue des Herbes market—thus saving time-strapped pilgrims a side trip to the Jordan valley. Ultimately these palm-cross souvenirs became so intrinsically intertwined with Holy Land pilgrimage that, in English, people who had successfully completed the journey came to be called "palmers."

*

Over time, as Christianity spread northward and westward, relics and religious souvenirs from the Holy Land made their way into shrines and cathedrals throughout Europe. As many of these items existed in fragmentary form, it often became necessarily to label them: a monastery near Rome kept its Holy Land mementos in small silk sacks bearing labels such as "Soil Drenched With the Blood of Christ" and "From the Table Where He Ate With the Disciples"; an inscription on a fourth-century funerary table now on display in the Louvre declares that it contains "dust from the land of our redemption."

By the fourth century such relics were being used to consecrate churches in Rome, and by the late eighth century the second council of Nicaea had decreed that all new churches must be consecrated with holy relics (or, if that was not possible, to acquire relics at the first opportunity). Some of these sacred objects came from the Holy Land, while others commemorated local saints and martyrs (in Rome, for instance, cathedrals were erected over the tombs of Saint Peter and Saint Paul). Spain's Santiago de Compostela became a popular pilgrimage site after the purported relics of Saint James were discovered there in the early ninth century; Canterbury became a magnet for English pilgrims after Archbishop Thomas Becket was assassinated there in 1170. When the Muslim occupation of Jerusalem made Holy Land travel more uncertain, pilgrimages to Rome, Santiago, and Canterbury (and scores of similar regional basilicas) boomed.

As had been the case in Jerusalem, these regional shrines scrambled to protect both their relics and their edifices from the souvenir mania of overzealous pilgrims. At Mont-St.-Michel in France, religious travelers were encouraged to collect seashore rocks (many of which were then used to consecrate provincial churches when the pilgrims returned home). Similarly, at Santiago de Compostela, pilgrims arriving at the cathedral were directed onward to the Spanish coast, where the ritual of collecting cockleshells and attaching them to one's travel garments marked the symbolic completion of the journey.

By the end of the twelfth century, actual Spanish cockleshells began to be replaced by shell-shaped lead badges, which Santiago pilgrims could buy in the cathedral square (thus saving a trek to the coast) and sew onto their cloaks or traveling hats. Such pilgrim's badges had, in fact, become something of a fad by that point, with each major shrine boasting its own standardized badge design: at Canterbury, badges depicted the head of Saint Thomas between two swords; at Amiens, they were emblazoned with the skull of John the Baptist; at Mont-St.-Michel they showed Saint Michael presiding over souls at the last judgment. These badges could, in many jurisdictions, exempt the wearer from tolls and taxes—and some pilgrims believed they had the same magical healing powers as traditional relics. To some cynics, wearing pilgrim badges amounted to a pompous display of conspicuous piety: Erasmus lampooned them in his ironic *Colloquies*, and an enemy of France's Louis XI once ridiculed the king's superstitious predilection for kissing his pewter and lead pilgrim badges during moments of joy or uncertainty.

In time, the trade in pilgrim-badge souvenirs became so lucrative that enterprising merchants got in on the action. In fourteenth-century France, the Valon family amassed a fortune by cornering the market in the manufacture and sale of pilgrim badges at Rocamadour. The bishop of Tulle took a healthy cut of the Valon family profits, of course, much like the archbishop of Santiago skimmed funds from the sale of Spanish cockleshell badges around the same time. This was emblematic of the fact that relics in general were a huge part of the religious economy throughout the Middle Ages. High-profile pilgrimage artifacts could exponentially increase the flow of donations to a given cathedral—and across Europe relics were bought, sold, stolen, smuggled, and counterfeited in the manner of any high-value commodity.

The trade (and, at times, manufacture) of mythic and religious relics in the Mediterranean area predates the Christian era—as evidenced by the display of Aeneas's shield on the island of Samothrace, or the enshrinement of Orpheus's head on the island of Lesbos. The sacred-object economy of Christian Jerusalem dates back at least to the fourth century, when Saint Helena traveled the Holy Land building churches and acquiring relics of the True Cross. One century later, Saint Augustine complained of the bogus monks who wandered the Mediterranean seaboard hawking relics of dubious origin. According to Historian Jonathan Sumption (whose book *Pilgrimage* provides many of the anecdotes I've cited here), the European relic market had become professionalized by the ninth century, eventually coming to resemble—and presage—the dealings of post-Renaissance art collectors.

The most prolific relic connoisseurs of medieval times were the emperors of Byzantium, whose massive collection of religious mementos was in large part sold off to (and stolen in the service of) Western European interests after the fourth Crusade sacked Constantinople in 1204. The fourth Lateran council censured the upsurge in relic-vending as sacrilege, but official criticism did little to keep the Latin emperors of Constantinople from selling a chunk of the True Cross (to Louis IX of France) to pay off debts, or pawning the crown of thorns (to the Venetians) to fund a war against the Bulgars. Amid this thirteenth-century relic boom, clerical scholars struggled to verify which items were authentic; peasants' skeletons were passed off as those of saints, and duplicate relics (including multiple heads of John the Baptist) abounded in competing basilicas across Europe and the Near East.

The popular Christian fixation with pilgrimage began to fade in the fifteenth and sixteenth centuries—partly because of the emergent Reformation and Renaissance, and partly because church officials feared the layman obsession with relics had become idolatrous. By that time, one thousand years of pilgrimage and relic-veneration had essentially turned the major cathedrals of Europe into ritualized museum-exhibits, each stocked with all manner of divine mementos. Outside of churches, private pilgrimage souvenirs served as badges of honor and worldliness in an era when few Europeans traveled beyond the nearest fair or market town. As often as not, mementos from a journey to the Holy Land (or Rome, or Canterbury) were not displayed at home in the manner of modern souvenirs, but attached to a cord and worn about the neck as an amulet. Pope Gregory the Great kept souvenir shavings from the chains of Saint Peter in a crucifix-shaped pendant; humbler pilgrims wore glass vials filled with shrine dust or sacramental oil.

It's worth noting that one of the reasons the church eventually deemphasized the rite of pilgrimage is that—from the earliest days of Christendom—religious travelers tended to embrace the earthly joys of life away from home. The most famous literary account of pilgrimage in Middle English, Chaucer's *Canterbury Tales*, prefaces the journey not with declarations of Christian piety, but exuberant images of spring renewal and lighthearted companionship. The pilgrims' tales that follow can, at times, be downright raunchy—and while Chaucer's work is fictional, it draws on the realities of medieval life. Indeed, while pilgrimages served a spiritual purpose, they also freed the traveler from the social and religious repression of his or her home community. At times this could lead to sexual escapades and drunken debauchery, but just as often the pilgrim wanderings led to intellectual curiosity—a transgression many church officials considered more dangerous than fleshly desire.

By the late sixteenth century, intellectual curiosity had surpassed pilgrimage as the main motivation behind nonmilitary, noncommercial travel for upper-class Europeans—and the souvenirs these new wanderers brought home began to influence the way entire nations viewed the rest of the world.

Thomas Jefferson's wood-chip from
Shakespeare's chair, 1786

3 SOUVENIRS IN THE AGE OF ENLIGHTENMENT

In April of 1786, Thomas Jefferson and John Adams, who were serving as diplomats in France and Britain at the time, embarked on a sightseeing tour of England. After traveling from London through Oxford and Blenheim they arrived at Stratford-Upon-Avon, which, in his diary, Adams reverentially called "the Scene of the Birth, Death and Sepulcher of Shakespeare." After tipping some local servants to gain access to the Bard's tomb and birthplace, the two American statesmen did something that to the modern imagination smacks of adolescent-grade vandalism: taking turns with a pocket knife, Jefferson and Adams each carved chunks from an antique chair alleged to have belonged to Shakespeare, and took the wood shavings home as souvenirs.

This incident illustrates how, by the Age of Enlightenment, the compulsion to collect travel keepsakes still echoed the rites of pilgrimage, even as the object of reverence had shifted from divinity and sainthood to art, science, and humanistic inquiry. In some ways, the seeds of the Enlightenment lay in the earlier epoch of medieval wandering, since pilgrims sought not just relics and religious souvenirs, but natural objects—ostrich eggs, porcupine quills, mummified dragon wings—that bore witness to the wonders and omens of God's creation. These items were often exhibited alongside traditional relics in the churches and cathedrals of Europe: a whale jawbone was displayed at Arezzo Cathedral in Tuscany; a mammoth tibia at Stephansdom in Vienna; a meteorite at Ensisheim in Alsace; and a stuffed crocodile at the Cathedral of Saint Mary in Seville. Initially displayed without being fully understood, these mementos of nature eventually came to be regarded less as relics than as specimens.

Indeed, the medieval Crusades and pilgrim wanderings that had informed Europe's understanding of the outside world eventually gave way to secular-minded expeditions that pioneered a sea route around Africa, stumbled across the Americas, and repeatedly underscored the fact that Jerusalem was not—as had previously been asserted—the center of the world. Travelers who might once have been compelled to collect dust from the tombs of saints began instead to seek out mementos of natural, scientific, and cultural-historical wonder. As more of the world was explored, objects were sought less for veneration than for information. Formal disciplines like ethnography and zoology did not yet exist, but all manner of exotica and *naturalia*—each with its own story of presumed function and origin—began to flow into cities like Venice, Paris, Amsterdam, Uppsala, and Oxford.

As had been the case with the religious relic trade of previous centuries, collecting and displaying these worldly curiosities became an aristocratic pursuit. Although noblemen throughout Europe sought to acquire such exotica in the sixteenth and seventeenth centuries, it was particularly fashionable among Germanic princes, who maintained *Wunderkammern* (wonder chambers)—small, museum-like rooms filled with curious objects and artifacts. An adviser to Christian I of Saxony outlined three categories of objects (art, animal specimens, and foreign curiosities) indispensable to *Wunderkammern*, though in practice the content of a given collection was simply meant to impress visitors. Depending on the resources and whims of the owner, a wonder chamber might contain mineral specimens and animal skins, exotic weapons and Ming porcelain, clockwork automata and primitive sculpture, sea corals and antique scrolls.

Most noblemen's *Wunderkammern* featured keepsakes of its owner's travels, but these chambers weren't considered souvenir collections so much as advertisements of status and importance. Whereas wealth and opulence had always been intrinsic to aristocratic lifestyles, wonder chambers enabled princes to present themselves as worldly sophisticates, masters of nature and history, champions of commerce and conquest. Because a given nobleman could only travel so much, the vogue for *Wunderkammern* objects meant that a far-flung network of traders, merchants, and explorers essentially became purchasing agents for commercialized exotica.

As natural and cultural curiosities were gathered, itemized, and analyzed in cities around Europe, *Wunderkammern* (and similar aristocratic and merchant-class souvenir collections) became repositories of practical knowledge and intellectual inquiry. Comparing wonder-chamber objects and drawing empirical parallels gave rise to a more scientific way of thinking about the outside world. Bogus animal specimens, such as the mummified "dragon wings" that once made their way into medieval relic collections, were studied for their artistry, even as they were determined to have been made from, say, dried ray skin and mastiff bones. According to historian Paula Findlen, this emergent sense of critical-mindedness underscored the way European thinking was shifting:

> In the early decades of the sixteenth century, [fake dragons] were sufficiently charged with religious meaning that it would have been heretical to suggest that they were anything less than God's will. By the 1550s, it had become possible to inspect these portents as examples of nature's variety and to suggest that human intervention made them approximate people's fantasies of a terrifying nature. Increasingly, such objects seemed to evoke pleasure rather than horror. . . . One wanted to know *how* they were made while avoiding the question of whether they existed.

In time, as the secular relics of travel broadened Europe's sense of the natural and cultural world, travel itself became an intrinsic part of aristocratic education—particularly in England, where "grand tours" of the continent became *de rigueur* during the Age of Enlightenment.

*

Of all the diaries and correspondence that came out of Britain during the Grand Tour era, the most memorable compendium of travel advice was written by the fourth Earl of Chesterfield, Philip Stanhope, whose teenaged son spent four years journeying through Europe in the mid-eighteenth century. Lord Chesterfield, who had himself taken a continental Grand Tour a generation earlier, was keen to instruct his son in gentlemanly ways. Good character, he asserted, was more important than fashion gestures, local inquiry more useful than sightseeing, and intellectual curiosity more productive than rote learning. Among the many frivolous and vulgar pursuits the nobleman warned against in Italy and France (including mindless entertainments, low-class taverns, and the company of harlots), Lord Chesterfield advises his son not to travel "knick-knackically." "Do not become a virtuoso of small wares . . . fooling away your money in baubles at toy shops," he asserts. "Have one handsome snuff-box and one handsome sword; but then no more pretty and very useless things."

Lord Chesterfield's advice is a prim reminder that (for all the emphasis Grand Tour patrons placed on high-class erudition and intellectual pilgrimage) the very act of coming into contact with new cultures and exotic experiences had a way of sending English student-travelers into a free-for-all spree of souvenir acquisition. A young Grand Tourist might collect tulip bulbs and porcelain in Holland, crystals and herbs in the Swiss Alps, scented soap and crystal-ware in Milan, and then sit for a keepsake portrait painted by the likes of Pompeo Battoni or Angelo Trevisani in Rome or Venice. In Paris, a shop called Noah's Ark offered travelers assorted *Wunderkammern*-style curiosities (shells, ivories, dried fishes, rare insects); in Naples, English demand for bits of ancient pottery and mosaic was so persistent that local artists began to forge and sell authentic-looking facsimiles. The most prolific souvenir shopper of the Grand Tour era was Richard Boyle, the third Earl of Burlington, who in 1715 returned from a one-year continental journey with 878 pieces of luggage.

For the most part, these Grand Tour souvenirs served as gifts, furnishings, and mementos upon a traveler's return to England, though in some cases they also formed the basis of ongoing scholarship. British awareness of Renaissance art in the seventeenth century, for example, owed a lot to Thomas Howard, the Earl of Arundel, who collected more than 700 paintings and drawings over the course of several Grand Tours. A century later, a wealthy country gentleman named Charles Townley turned his Italian Grand Tour into a lifelong obsession with Greco-Roman coinage and sculpture. Lord Arundel's art collection was bequeathed to Oxford University, while Townley's artifacts wound up in London's newly emergent British Museum, which had taken the old aristocratic concept of the *Wunderkammern* and made it public.

In a sense, the rise of the public museum refined the aura of travel objects, transforming their acquisition and display from a mostly private ritual to an increasingly collective one. The modern idea of the public museum traces its origins back to Sir Hans Sloane, a gentleman-scientist who, upon his death in 1753, entrusted his extensive collection of books, drawings, flora, fauna, and curiosities to the British nation. Though Sloane acquired some of these objects on journeys to France and Jamaica, most weren't travel souvenirs per se; a collector of collections, Sloan bought entire *Wunderkammern* from various European botanists, apothecaries, and clergymen. Sloan's 70,000 or so artifacts (including 40,000 books) formed the seed of the British Museum, which opened in 1759 and grew in tandem with an expansive era of travel, exploration, and conquest. Whereas in Wunderkammern the specimens on display spoke to the wealth, sophistication, and power of its owner, the objects in the British Museum spoke to the wealth, sophistication, and power of an entire nation.

It's worth noting here that, while many of the objects exhibited in public institutions like the British Museum may have originated as souvenirs of a sort, the very act of institutional enshrinement turned them into something different. If by its very etymology the word "souvenir" is connected to remembrance, an object displayed in a museum serves a different kind of memory. To a Grand Tourist like Charles Townley, the sight of a terra-cotta figurine might call to mind the sensual and emotional associations of a spring afternoon in the Sicilian countryside; to a museum visitor, that same terra-cotta figurine—now catalogued, labeled, and placed in a glass case alongside three dozen other Greco-Roman ceramics—served a more abstract notion of history and culture. By replacing the object's private/associative narrative with a public/interpretive one, what was collected as a souvenir ceased to function as a souvenir in its original sense.

*

Over the course of the late eighteenth and early nineteenth centuries, the objects in the British Museum were organized and classified to further scholarly research, but they also wound up fueling the Romantic imagination. Vital as it was to advancements in the fields of ethnology and archaeology, the museum's collection was just as renowned for influencing John Keats's "Ode on a Grecian Urn" (and the poem's ecstatic assertion that "beauty is truth, truth beauty"). Regarded in their original context, the objects that made their way into the museum bore witness to natural wonder or artistic achievement; viewed as a whole—alongside hundreds of other exotic artifacts in an era before mass communication—these objects were regarded as an enchanting index of the world's possibilities.

One of Keats's lesser-known poems, "On Seeing a Lock of Milton's Hair," is an interesting window into the Romantic worldview that had captured the imagination of England's intelligentsia at the time. While the poem itself is a meditation on the elusive nature of greatness, its backstory is more telling than its content. As it happened, locks of Milton's hair were in circulation in England in the early nineteenth century thanks to a feat of grave robbery that had gone down in 1790. At the time, London's St Giles-without-Cripplegate Church was undergoing renovations in anticipation of erecting a memorial over the tomb of the *Paradise Lost* poet, who had died 116 years earlier. When a coffin thought to have been Milton's was identified, a group of souvenir-mad locals stole into the church, smashed the coffin open, and made off with the corpse's hair (and most of its teeth).

The fact that Keats eventually came into contact a lock of Milton's pilfered hair underscores the Romantic-era fixation with individual greatness and the outsized aura of history. Though locks of hair had for generations been kept as an affectionate token for remembering lovers, family members, and the occasional public figure, seeking to connect with greatness through corporeal keepsakes was something of a craze in Keats's day. During his Grand Tour sojourn in Milan, for instance, Keats's contemporary Lord Byron was inspired to steal "one shining strand" of hair belonging to Renaissance-era femme fatale Lucrezia Borgia. Around the same time, diarist Henry Crabb Robinson was so taken with the British victory at Waterloo that he had a dentist replace his rotten molar with a souvenir tooth harvested from the battlefield. (Keats's own personal effects were preserved after his death; a plait of his hair now resides in Oxford's Bodleian Library.)

The emergence of Romanticism can, in fact, help explain the actions of Thomas Jefferson and John Adams during their visit to Stratford-Upon-Avon in 1786. One century earlier Shakespeare-tourism scarcely existed in Stratford, but as the English fixation with individual genius took hold in the eighteenth century, efforts were made to compile the Bard's biography, annotate his plays, and enshrine his place of birth. The word "souvenir" was just emerging in English to refer to a "token of remembrance" (Barnhart's *Dictionary of Etymology* dates its use to 1782), but the act of carving a sliver from Shakespeare's chair was, at the time, as much an attempt to commune with the Bard's aura as it was to commemorate a moment of travel. Jefferson and Adams hadn't traveled to Stratford with the intention to deface Shakespeare's property; they were just participating in a common tourist ritual.

Even then, the American statesmen left Stratford feeling skeptical about what they had experienced. Jefferson's journal entry expresses irritation at having to pay for each aspect of the experience ("seeing his tomb, 1 shilling; entertainment, 4 shillings; servants, 2 shillings"), and he later quipped that, "like the relics of the saints," Shakespeare's chair "must miraculously reproduce itself." For Adams, being allowed to cut chips from the chair compensated for the fact that there was no real interpretive information about the Bard's estate. "There is nothing preserved of this great genius which is worth knowing," he wrote. "Nothing which might inform us what education, what company, what accident turned his mind to letters and the drama. His name is not even on his grave stone." What became of Adams's Shakespearian wood chip is not known; Jefferson's is now on display in his old bedroom at Monticello.

The Romantic reverence that made secular saints out of people like Shakespeare soon took hold across the Atlantic, and when Jefferson and Adams died in 1826, their own belongings took on the aura of sacred objects. The most exalted of America's Founding Fathers was George Washington, whose Mount Vernon estate in Virginia became the site of patriotic pilgrimage not long after his death in 1799. At first the flow of travelers was modest, and guests' compulsion to pluck strands of ivy and pry splinters of molding from Washington's mansion yielded minor, manageable damage. By the 1850s, however, the emergence of railroad travel led to a surge in everyday visitors to Mount Vernon. As more and more of the estate was carted off by tourists eager to possess a tangible connection to the founding president's life, Washington's cash-strapped descendants struggled to keep the estate in good repair.

The Mount Vernon situation reflected the challenges inherent in preserving the young nation's monuments as mid-century industrialization and transportation improvements fueled a middle-class tourism boom. In the 1830s, for example, breaking off pieces of Plymouth Rock in Massachusetts was such a common practice that a nearby grocery kept a hammer and chisel on hand for tourists who'd forgotten to bring their own. By 1859 the landmark had deteriorated so noticeably that local officials had made it illegal to hammer off chunks (though this was a theoretical deterrent at best, and, in 1880, what was left of Plymouth Rock was cordoned off entirely from public access).

Pragmatic efforts to protect Mount Vernon from relic-hunters began in the early 1850s, when caretakers harvested several acres of the estate's timber, which was then used to fashion souvenir canes, gavels, tobacco boxes, picture frames, and axe handles. The manufacture of such keepsakes generated funds that could be used to renovate the estate, but these wooden objects also served as a deterrent against the theft and vandalism that had characterized an earlier generation of souvenir hunting. When, in 1853, the Mount Vernon Ladies' Association was created to purchase and protect the property, the concept of a "gift shop" was central to the group's strategy to keep visitors from defacing historical artifacts. In time, the gift shop diversified its selection of local-wood keepsakes (which are still sold at Mount Vernon) with items such as leather-bound history books, patriotic tchotchkes, jars of honey, and reproductions of colonial-era jewelry and china.

Mount Vernon would go on to serve as the national model for historical preservation and the strategic curation of tourist sites—though the popular practice of acquiring souvenirs by way of casual plunder and vandalism thrived into the twentieth century. During the 1876 American Centennial, for example, tourists visiting the Capitol snipped off swatches of the gallery curtains (and carved off chunks of the Speaker's desk) in the House of Representatives. When the White House was renovated in 1902, so many souvenir-hunters showed up to snatch discarded lathe and plasterwork that officials had to ban visitors from the construction site. One decade later, when the original Star-Spangled Banner was donated to the Smithsonian, its scarred appearance owed not to the bombardment of Fort McHenry in 1814, but to the scores of patriotic souvenir-hunters who had clipped off what amounted 20 percent of the massive flag's fabric over the course of the nineteenth century.

One year before the Star-Spangled Banner arrived in the Smithsonian, the *Washington Post*, in an editorial entitled "The Dire Souvenir Mania," expressed concern at the seeming destructiveness of middle-class tourist habits. "The business of gathering souvenirs has become a national mania before whose fury many of the great monuments of the earth are fast melting away," the article noted. "Not even the monuments of our own illustrious dead are safe from the impious hands of these souvenir-seeking vandals."

Though the article's tone of alarm was well earned, America's souvenir habits had by then begun to shift into a less damaging direction. Manufactured trinkets and mass-market tchotchkes, which provided a cheap alternative to ransacking historical sites for keepsakes, were on the rise by the end of the nineteenth century. In 1903 Washington's Pennsylvania Avenue featured some thirty souvenir kiosks, most of which sold cheap, factory-made mementos manufactured in Germany. Though some patriotic tourists grumbled about buying imported trinkets in their own nation's capital, the kiosks did good business, and damage to area monuments declined accordingly.

By the end of the twentieth century, imported keepsakes were accepted as the norm in tourist areas worldwide, and mass-produced souvenirs had grown into a multibillion-dollar global industry.

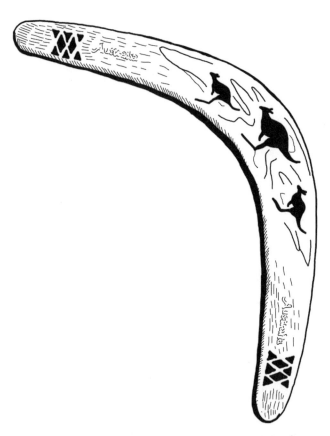

Gift shop boomerang, author's collection, 2006

4 INTERLUDE: MUSEUMS OF THE PERSONAL

I learned a curious lesson about the subjectivity of souvenirs at age fifteen, not long after I came across the remnants of a plane crash while hiking through the Front Range of the Colorado Rockies. The wreckage, which was strewn along the slopes of a pine-studded ridge near Ormes Peak, belonged to a B-24 Liberator long-range bomber that had gone down in stormy weather the night of April 26, 1944, killing its seven-man crew.

When I first saw the twisted bits of wing and fuselage half-buried amid tan-pink chunks of granite on the mountainside, I was taken by the unadorned gravitas of the spectacle. I recall sifting through the smaller bits of debris, gripped with naïve jitters—half apprehensive, half hopeful—at the prospect of finding human remains. To my relief (and mild disappointment) I didn't find any bleached bones or yellowed teeth—though I did find a small, rusted aviation fuse box, which I scavenged as a souvenir to show to friends when I went back home to Kansas.

To my chagrin, none of my Kansas friends took much interest in the old fuse box. Whereas I could look at it and recall the solemn spectacle of a shattered Second World War-era bomber littering a mountain slope, my friends saw little more than a corroded piece of metal about half the size of a cigarette pack. To me, it evoked an aura of young men (not much older than we were) plunging to their deaths on a lonely mountain ridge; to my friends, it looked a rusty bit of junk that could have once belonged to anything.

Part of the problem here was that I hadn't done a very good job of explaining the plane crash itself. Whereas in retrospect I can go online and look up the circumstances of the crash—plane model, death count, the exact date of the incident—at the time I had only the vaguest sense for its specifics. Moreover, my friends knew that I hadn't just randomly stumbled across a plane crash in the Colorado Rockies; I had been hiking there, along with a half-dozen other teenage boys and a college-aged trail guide, as part of a Christian summer camp I attended each summer. If there had been any uncertainty or stakes-filled tension in the experience, it had come from the fact my camp-counselor had implored us not to take souvenirs from the crash site. I had surreptitiously pocketed the fuse box in the hopes of sharing the grim emotional energy of the site with my friends, only to discover that a solitary fuse box didn't mean much away from the rest of the wreckage.

In all fairness, I can't recall having taken much interest in my friends' travel mementos at that age, and this disconnect—that is, the inability of most travel objects to evoke an intuitive sense of provenance and significance to people who weren't there—is why souvenirs inevitably carry a personal resonance that can't be replicated at a broader social level.

This very conundrum made it difficult, over the years, for the curators of museums and *Wunderkammern* to instill a sense of appreciation and understanding in everyday visitors, who—much of the time—weren't really sure what it was they were seeing. When Peter the Great's sprawling Kunstkamera museum was opened to the public in 1727, for instance, commoners had to be enticed into the exhibits with free shots of vodka. Around the same time, in England, curiosity collections were often acquired and displayed in barbershops or coffee houses, where the display items served to titillate (and attract customers) more than inform and enlighten.

Even members of the European aristocracy, who in principle supported the scientific mission of museums, had doubts about the subjective nature of the items on display. When antiquarian Horace Walpole was bequeathed trusteeship of the British Museum in 1753, for instance, he made no secret of the fact that he considered it little more than one man's collection of random esoterica. "You will scarce guess how I employ my time," he quipped in a letter to a friend. "Chiefly at present in the guardianship of embryos and cockleshells. Sir Hans Sloane is dead, and has made me one of the trustees to his museum. . . . He valued it at fourscore thousand—and so would anybody who loves hippopotamuses, sharks with one ear, and spiders as big as geese."

Walpole's disdain for Sloane's biological specimens is telling, since in principle he had no bias against the act of collecting itself. A little more than one decade earlier, while on his own Grand Tour of the continent, Walpole had succumbed to the same kind of souvenir mania that gripped so many of his young English contemporaries. "I am far gone in medals, lamps, idols, prints, and all the small commodities to the purchase of which I can attain," he wrote from Rome in 1741. "I would buy the Coliseum if I could." If Walpole later saw Sloane's British Museum specimens to be trifling and uninspired, it's because his own collecting habits centered on art and history rather than the natural world. Over time the British Museum (and institutions like it) moved past the subjective fixations of its early trustees by systematically diversifying its collections and broadening its emphasis on objective interpretive information for the wider public.

In a sense, the souvenirs I've collected at various stages of my life have constituted a haphazard museum of my own way of looking at, being in, and making sense of the world. Unlike a more formal museum, nothing is ever labeled and I don't use a system that dictates which items will be displayed, or where, or for how long. With the exception of the masks I bought during my early years in Asia, none of my travel mementos have been collected in a systematic or sequential way. They have, rather, been acquired in spontaneous moments of inspiration, for reasons I sometimes have trouble describing later. To accumulate souvenirs in a more systematic way would, for me, be at odds with the joy of collecting souvenirs on impulse.

I suspect my way of collecting souvenirs is normal. A popular bromide about travel mementos is that they are a form of conspicuous consumption, exotic conversation pieces that give us a pretext to hold forth on our far-flung travels in the company of friends and acquaintances. This notion—that souvenirs are somehow status objects aimed at other people—might well hold true for certain meticulous, self-conscious nouveau riche travelers, but I'd reckon people collect their most meaningful and enduring souvenirs in ways that are surprising, even to themselves. We might collect and curate our books, vinyl records, or even antiques in ways that easily make sense to other people, but our most personal travel souvenirs have a way of defying easy classification.

A short section of wall near a north-looking window in my living room, for instance, features a wooden boomerang and three Aboriginal dot paintings I purchased in and around Alice Springs in 2005. At first glance, they look like a fairly typical collection of travel mementos from a journey to central Australia; look a little closer, and they reveal themselves as the cheaper sort of souvenirs one might buy in that part of the world. The dot paintings are quite basic, with no individual flourishes on the part of the artist; the boomerang (which I now realize was probably made in China) is nonfunctional and features machine-painted kangaroos. Look at this section of my living room wall, and you'll recognize the kinds of items a person might buy after a few minutes in any Alice Springs gift shop; these are items that, to all appearances simply say, "I went to central Australia."

When I look at the wall, however, I don't typically think about Australia. I was, at the time, visiting the country on magazine assignment to do a story about Aboriginal tourism initiatives, and while I enjoyed the trip (and was proud of the story I wrote), I didn't experience the country in an open-ended, openhearted way. I was mainly there as a reporter, and the souvenirs were bought in haste. Moreover, Australia didn't have the same emotional impact on me as South Korea, which I had visited en route to Sydney and Alice Springs. Pusan, Korea, where I'd once spent two formative years of my twenties teaching English, had been a much more memorable experience—mainly because it was the first time I'd returned in nearly ten years, and I was taken by all the changes I saw there. I didn't think to buy souvenirs in Pusan because, in a way, I knew the place too well; weirdly, getting inexpensive paintings and boomerangs near Alice Springs was a kind of placeholder, a way of remembering Korea as well as Australia.

A final twist here lies in the fact that, earlier in 2005, I had come to own a home in Kansas—the first house I could really call my own. I had already hung up the Asian masks I had collected (and then stopped collecting) in my early days of world travel, and I wanted to add a new cultural texture as I remodeled my house. That I bought Aboriginal dot paintings in Australia was thus connected to the novelty of possessing a wall where they would hang. My boomerang and dot paintings don't simply evoke Australia (and Korea) when I look at them; weirdly, they also remind me of the understated pride I felt the year I came to own a house in Kansas.

Walk through my house now and you'll see all manner of happenstance (almost accidental) souvenir displays, little museums of the personal, that evoke private associations I could probably never communicate with any effectiveness to people who haven't directly shared in my life experiences. One travel memento I have on display is a 1980s-era topographical quadrangle map depicting a section of El Paso County, Colorado. It hangs innocuously alongside other maps in the mud room at the back of my house, and in a certain sense it's interesting for the bygone elegance of its artistry and the secret language of its logic—the way its curved lines evoke abstractions that can be made concrete only on backcountry trails (with the help of another bygone technology, the compass).

When I look at this topographical map I don't just think of old orienteering technology, or that small section of Colorado; instead, I think of the wreckage of the B-24 Liberator near Ormes Peak, and how I felt when I first saw it at age fifteen.

As it happened, the way my friends reacted to the rusty aviation fuse box planted a seed of regret that took root and blossomed in the years that followed. For some reason, I couldn't look at the fuse box without the sense that I had somehow desecrated the scene of the crash by taking home a part of it. In the months after I first brought it home to Kansas, I removed it from the collection of souvenirs I kept in my bedroom and put it into a box in my closet. But I didn't feel right keeping it there, either—and, four years after plucking the plane-crash remnant from a distant mountainside, I put it into my backpack and took it back to Colorado.

By that point I had become a counselor at that same summer camp. It was now my job to lead teenagers through the Colorado wilderness, and (when the occasion was appropriate) to show them the site of the B-24 plane crash. One August afternoon in 1990, when I was doing just that, I unceremoniously placed the fuse box back amid the wreckage I'd sifted through four years earlier. As a souvenir, it hadn't just failed to inspire the imaginations of my friends; it had left me feeling unsettled by the notion that it didn't really belong to me.

Now, if I want to remind myself of the person I was in the summer of my fifteenth year, I can simply walk out to the topographical map in my mud room, trace my finger along its curved lines, and (on my own, private terms) dream myself back into the moment that made the place meaningful to me.

Salem Witch souvenir spoon, 1891

5 SOUVENIRS IN THE AGE OF MECHANICAL REPRODUCTION

America's social critics had never been fond of souvenirs, and this distaste only grew as middle-class tourists began to seek out factory-made knickknacks as travel keepsakes. In March of 1906, writer John Walker Harrington declared that America's growing obsession with mass-produced souvenirs was turning the country into a nation of nitwits. Coining the satirical phrase "postal carditis" in an article for *American Magazine*, Walker bemoaned how an "incipient mania for cherishing the useless" was making America into a frivolous place. "Postal carditis and allied collecting manias are working havoc among the inhabitants of the United States," he wrote. "The germs of these maladies, brought to this country in the baggage of tourists, escaped quarantine regulations, and were propagated with amazing rapidity.

Unless such manifestations are checked, millions of persons of now normal lives and irreproachable habits will become victims of faddy degeneration of the brain."

Harrington's chagrin at postcards and other manufactured souvenirs revealed how much travel had changed since the days of the aristocratic Grand Tour. Whereas a souvenir once spoke to the relative wealth and privilege required to travel great distances, the rise of railroads, steamships, and industrial manufacturing meant that souvenirs now reflected middle-class, mass-market sensibilities. A traveler of previous generations might have brought home an Andalusian tapestry with the full confidence that his high-class peers possessed the erudition to recognize its origins; a modern bourgeois tourist advertised a similar journey by mailing home cheap picture postcards of Andalusian cathedrals. An aristocratic tourist might have identified her vase as Milanese by the quality of its crystal; a middle-class globetrotter knew her ceramic plate was Milanese because it was embossed with the word "Milan."

In his book *The Tourist: A New Theory of the Leisure Class*, sociologist Dean MacCannell notes that this middle-class travel sensibility had become common in European cities by the year 1900: "The special reasons for travel (to visit a friend, fair, ceremony, or religious shrine, to do business or research, to shop for a special article), were giving way to the modern idea that no reason need be given to visit [a place] except to see the city itself and its sights." As a newly mobile class of people expanded the definition of travel, souvenirs themselves became more mobile. Local artifacts gave way to branded tchotchkes—brass medallions, pewter mugs, glass tumblers—that had often been manufactured elsewhere. Tourists began to collect sets of such knickknacks to showcase and recall their far-flung travels, and gift shops standardized their offerings accordingly. Popular as these inexpensive souvenirs were, cultural critics like Harrington dismissed them as ersatz junk, and by the 1920s the term *kitsch*—a German word previously applied to cheap, sentimental art—was being used in English to describe mass-produced tourist keepsakes.

If one were to pinpoint a single moment when souvenirs came of age as an organized, globally minded American industry, it might well be the World's Columbian Exposition of 1893, which attracted 28 million visitors to Chicago over the course of six months. Among the many keepsakes on offer to commemorate the event (including posters, buttons, booklets, medallions, and jewelry), the most popular souvenir items that year proved to be commemorative teaspoons, which were sold by the tens of thousands. Since the expo honored the 400th anniversary of Europeans' arrival in the New World, the highest-selling spoons were embossed with images of Christopher Columbus, Queen Isabella, or the *Santa Maria*; other spoons honored the invention of the Ferris wheel, the achievements of women, and the city of Chicago. By the time the expo shut its gates in October of that year, contemporary newspapers had declared that the nation was in the grips of a "souvenir spoon craze."

As it happened, the craze for souvenir teaspoons in the 1890s was the result of a calculated strategy on the part of American jewelers and silversmiths. In 1891, two years before the Chicago World's Fair, the Jewelers' Circular Company of New York published a promotional booklet called *Souvenir Spoons of America*, which characterized its subject as a fad waiting to happen. "From Maine to California, from Minnesota to Florida," it announced, "the cry is for souvenir spoons." That same year, a silversmiths' merchandise catalogue insinuated that collecting souvenir spoons had already become a tourist trend. "It has become the practice now to obtain a spoon from each place that one may visit," the introduction text read, "preserving a souvenir of a happy outing, or a delightful recollection of a pleasant locality, or the remembrance of a distinguished man or historical spot."

In a savvy attempt to associate spoon-collecting with refined Old-World customs, *Souvenir Spoons of America* detailed how Daniel Low, a jeweler from Salem, Massachusetts, had in 1890 traveled to Holland and Germany, where he'd noticed that the fashion among European travelers was to buy a souvenir spoon from each city they visited. Inspired, Mr. Low came home and designed a spoon that commemorated the historic witchcraft trials of his hometown. When Low's Salem Witch spoon ended up selling in the thousands of dollars that year, other American jewelers and silversmiths began to patent and promote souvenir spoons of their own. These early successes were catalyzed by the spoon trade at the Chicago World's Fair;

by the end of that decade souvenir teaspoons had become a standard fixture in gift shops nationwide, and jewelry-manufacturing towns like Attleboro, Massachusetts, were prospering from the boom.

Curiously, the supposed European fashion for souvenir spoons had itself been invented by the very tradesmen who sought to profit from it. Historically, small spoons had been made to commemorate events like weddings and baptisms as early as the seventeenth century. By the early nineteenth century, decorative teaspoons were sold alongside seals, pennants, buttons, and fobs as keepsakes of historical anniversaries and school graduations; London's 1851 Crystal Palace Exhibition featured a special-edition spoon that commemorated the event. When Daniel Low traveled to Europe in 1890, however, the notion that each continental locality should regale tourists with its own branded souvenir spoons only went back one year, to the 1889 Paris Exposition Universelle, where German silversmiths had popularized the idea through their own exhibits and circulars.

In addition to promoting the idea of collectible spoons, the 1889 Paris Exposition sold rudimentary versions of future gift-shop staples such as snow globes and collectible thimbles. The expo is perhaps best remembered for the debut of the Eiffel Tower—the tallest man-made structure in the world at the time—and this occasion was commemorated by all manner of keepsakes, including etched crystal glasses, painted ceramic serving plates, and copper admission tokens engraved with an image of the tower's height compared to such iconic world structures as the Washington Monument and the Great Pyramid of Giza.

Of all the souvenirs to find a new audience at the Paris Expo that year, however, the most significant was the picture postcard. Postal cards had existed in primitive form in previous decades, and as early as the 1870s one could buy mailing cards decorated with sentimental or patriotic images. What the Paris Exposition (and, soon thereafter, the Chicago World's Fair) popularized was the idea that picture postcards could be printed to commemorate a specific event or location. Collectors responded, as did entrepreneurs, and as postcard mailing prices went down (in tandem with improved photolithography and collotypography techniques), picture postcards went through a popular "craze" of their own. By 1906 the total volume of mail in the United States had gone up by thirty-five percent, and the *Post Card Dealer* was reporting sales of 750 million in Great Britain and more than a billion in Germany. People in Sweden, a country of just five million people at the time, mailed more than forty-eight million postcards in 1904. The postcard industry became so powerful that in 1909, US legislators passed the Payne-Aldrich Tariff Act, meant to protect the interests of domestic printers against German imports.

Postcards may well be the most influential souvenir item to emerge from the late nineteenth century. Part object, part information, picture postcards were cheap, mobile, self-contained, and easy to collect. The picture on the front of the card advertised the act of travel, and the postmark on the back certified it as authentic. In an era before the availability of inexpensive snapshot cameras, postcards became a powerful medium for evoking what various corners of the world looked like, and how one might interact with them. Postcard entrepreneurs popularized notions of what sights were worth seeing in a given location, and postcard artists and photographers presented idealized visions of how it should be seen. Even as point-and-shoot snapshots gradually replaced postcards over the course of the twentieth century, tourist photographs tended to mimic the visual clichés of postcard images (a trend that has persisted into the age of digital photos and social media).

The popularity of postcards and collectible teaspoons is emblematic of just how radically the notion of a souvenir changed in the industrial era. At the beginning of the nineteenth century, travel souvenirs were usually artifacts, found objects, or place-specific keepsakes created by local craftsmen; by the end of the century, souvenirs were just as likely to be mass-produced gift-shop items that depended upon increasingly sophisticated networks of manufacturers, distributors, and vendors. American travel entrepreneurs like Henry Flagler and Fred Harvey used the promise of colorful and trendy souvenirs as part of their marketing efforts to lure railroad tourists to Florida and the American Southwest. Tourist gift shops became more innovative in their attempts to increase revenues, selling not just teaspoons and postcards, but teaspoon display racks and postcard-collection albums. Later, as interest in teaspoons waned and the rise of snapshot photography reduced the demand for postcards, manufacturers and vendors collaborated to intuit—and influence—which souvenir products new generations of tourists might want to buy.

*

Souvenir teaspoons are still sold in the United States, with supply companies like Dutch American Import of Bend, Oregon, catering to various museum stores and national park gift shops. According to Marshall Lundgren, the company's vice president, Dutch American's various lines of souvenir spoons (including rhinestone spoons, cameo spoons, charm spoons, fluted spoons, demitasse spoons, totem spoons, and dinner bells) sell about 25,000 units a year. Two generations ago, Dutch American sold five times that many teaspoons, but an ongoing decline in market demand means the company has now diversified its offerings to include decorative whiskey flasks, inlaid pint glasses, vintage-style pocket watches, money clips, letter openers, and pocket knives. "Spoons don't sell like they used to, but I don't think people will ever stop asking for them," Lundgren told me. "I guess it's a tradition thing. Somebody's great-grandmother collected them, so they've decided they're going to do the same."

I met Lundgren—and dozens of souvenir-industry professionals like him—at the Las Vegas Souvenir & Resort Gift Show, the industry's biggest trade event, which sprawls out across the Las Vegas Convention Center for several days each September. Here, representatives from more than 1300 souvenir suppliers showcase their latest designs and products to buyers from American resort hotels, cruise lines, wineries, spas, amusement parks, beach shops, state parks, zoos, aquariums, botanical gardens, hospitals, college bookstores, and sports stadiums. As is the case at similar trade fairs in Europe and Asia, industry suppliers work in tandem with retailers and manufacturers to develop and market travel keepsakes that tourists will find appealing. At stake is a portion of a US souvenir and gift market that generates $19 billion of revenue each year.

Using the Vegas Souvenir & Resort Gift Show's 229-page vendor catalog as a guidebook, I wandered the 2016 event for three days, talking to exhibitors who'd come there to promote the latest in souvenir magnets, coffee mugs, key chains, T-shirts, hats, shot glasses, toothpick holders, pencil sharpeners, ashtrays, license plates, holiday ornaments, candles, wind chimes, hand towels, plush toys, puzzles, and candy. Whereas my previous experiences with souvenir vendors were rooted to specific travel locations, the men and women I met at the Vegas show dealt in a world of abstraction and hypothesis, each of them hoping to develop and sell products that might appeal to dozens of different destinations at once.

Most of the exhibitors I met worked for small, family-run operations that had, over the years, learned to adapt with the times and introduce new products on a trial-and-error basis. Sea to Sky Photography primarily focused on custom-made souvenir card decks, for example, but its owner had recently branched out into what he called "Snow to Go," a packet of superabsorbent powdered polymer that gets cold and fluffy when you combine it with water. Some vendors, such as Freakers USA (which crowd-funded its line of novelty socks in 2015), were new to the souvenir business; others, like Parris Manufacturing Company (which debuted its line of toy cap guns in 1936), had been in business for generations. An exhibitor whose business card identified him as the "Senior Penny Guy" dealt in machines that press coins into elongated, custom-designed medallions—a souvenir technology that dates back to the 1893 Chicago World's Fair. Elsewhere, several wholesalers offered vinyl-encased insects and arachnids—a product that has proven so successful over the years that special farms have been set up in China to grow scorpions, tarantulas, locusts, spiders, mantises, and stag beetles to supply the souvenir paperweight market.

No single buyer or exhibitor I met claimed to have an all-encompassing understanding of the souvenir industry, but talking to dozens of them over the course of three days did give me a sense for the basics. Most souvenirs, I learned, are designed to be eye-catching, small in size, easily portable, not too fragile, and not too expensive. Travelers often don't think about souvenir purchases until they walk into a gift shop, so qualities like attractiveness, simplicity, novelty, or humor are meant to inspire an impulse buy. Printing the destination's name on an item (known in the industry as "name-dropping") also makes it more appealing to potential buyers—especially on objects that are readily collectible, like magnets, pins, patches, mugs, and shot glasses. Men and women are equally likely to buy souvenirs on a journey, though women tend to spend more money on gifts. First-time visitors are more likely to buy souvenirs than veteran travelers, and lower-income tourists make more purchases than well-heeled tourists (though wealthy folks make up for this by favoring more expensive boutique items). Packaging can do as much to sell an item as the item itself, especially when it comes to food products like candy.

Another important industry consideration is the "souvenir year," which begins around Labor Day, as vendors begin to make plans for the next summer's high season. I learned this from Skip Smith, whose company Smith-Western bills itself as "The Nation's Premier Supplier for the Tourist Attraction Industry Since 1947." Smith-Western had a large booth at the front of the convention center showroom, and when I first met Skip he was discussing souvenir-design ideas with a buyer from Kennedy Space Center in Florida. Skip explained how the preliminary ideas he was discussing with the client would eventually go to designers in his art department, who would fine-tune the idea and create a sample for the customer. Once that was approved, Smith-Western would work with companies in China to manufacture the new souvenir items and pack them into container ships bound for the United States. "There's a reason why they hold this convention in September," he told me. "For importers the process has to start now, so the products will be ready by

April or May." Among Skip's more successful products in recent years was a children's "Junior Ranger" vest he made for clients like zoos and national parks. "That idea started out as a sketch on a napkin," he said. "Kids really use their imagination when they go places, so it's great when you can find an idea that caters to that."

Smith-Western traces its origins to Skip's father Kyle Smith, a Second World War veteran who began selling postcards out of a Mercury station in the late 1940s and expanded his business as the postwar economy grew. Like Kyle Smith, most souvenir suppliers in that era were essentially traveling salesmen, but by the 1950s various wholesalers had begun to band together and invite retail buyers to makeshift trade exhibitions at regional hotels. At first these events were informal, room-to-room operations that took place in a single motel hallway, but in the mid-1960s a pair of enterprising suppliers catalyzed the industry by creating a national souvenir trade convention in Gatlinburg, Tennessee. Called the Smoky Mountain Gift Show, the annual event grew in tandem with the rise of jet travel, and gave the American souvenir industry a sense of its own scope and potential. Business nationwide grew steadily for the next three decades, peaking at $25 billion in annual sales in 1998. Since then the emergence of online retailing and wholesaling has stagnated the American gift-shop market, though globally the industry is expected to expand as newly minted middle-class tourists from emergent economies like China and India begin to travel the world.

For all the ways that the commercial souvenir industry has grown complex and global, however, it still hinges on some fairly basic principles. One story multiple vendors told me in Las Vegas centered on the 2016 Rio Summer Games, where—despite all the planning that went into officially branded keepsakes—the hottest souvenir of the summer proved to be Skol Lager beverage cups depicting the various Olympic sports. Given the choice between $28 plastic mascot figurines and $46 polo shirts, Brazil's sports tourists were, in unexpectedly large numbers, electing to simply drink a $4 beer and keep the cup. Al Bass, a 79-year-old exhibitor who'd operated a souvenir-supply business out of Massachusetts since 1971, told me that the surest way to get things wrong was to overthink what tourists want. "Inexpensive and simple," he told me. "That's what people end up buying. Something with the name of the destination on it, something they can give as a gift or use for themselves when they get home." Statistically speaking, he added, T-shirts, hats, and cheap jewelry (including things like key chains and bottle openers) sell far more, year in and year out, than more imaginative or specialized keepsakes. "At the end of the day, people don't get too philosophical when they go to a big tourist destination," Bass said. "They just want something that proves they've been there."

9/11 Memorial gift-shop umbrella, 2014

6 SOUVENIRS AND HUMAN SUFFERING

Before we move on to explore the various ways travel keepsakes create meaning for the people who collect them in the twenty-first century, it's worth pointing out that the act of collecting souvenirs has not always been an innocent (if occasionally obnoxious) expression of curiosity, devotion, or remembrance. Among the more lighthearted examples of public desecration cited in the *Washington Post*'s 1911 "Dire Souvenir Mania" editorial, the writer includes mention of a murder that had happened just days earlier. "Horrible as it is to relate," the article notes, "many of the teeth and smaller bones of the negro lynched In Pennsylvania were carried away by citizens of Coatesville to be sacredly preserved as souvenirs of that ghastly event."

The *Post* was referring to the lynching of Zachariah Walker, a black itinerant worker who, having been accused of killing a white factory guard in a Pennsylvania steel town, was hauled out of police custody and burned alive in front of a crowd of three thousand people. According to *No Crooked*

Death, Dennis Downey and Raymond Hyser's book-length account of the incident, some in the crowd commemorated the event by carting off bits of Walker's corpse:

> Approximately one hundred and fifty individuals maintained an all-night vigil near the fire, waiting to collect souvenirs. Some of the more aggressive among them used fence railings to dredge Walker's bones from the glowing embers. The manacles and footboard were also pulled from the pyre and then doused in water and broken up as souvenirs. The next day, several enterprising boys even sold some of Walker's remains to anxious customers in Coatesville. A curious reporter who visited the lynching site several months later found many changes, including the absence of grass where the burning took place and the almost complete demolition of the split-rail fence. "Visitors have carried away anything that looked like a souvenir," he wrote.

As horrifying as this grisly ritual was, it was not unique. One decade earlier, in Newnan, Georgia, two thousand men, women, and children watched as the ears, fingers, heart, and liver were sliced from the lynched body of a black laborer named Sam Hose and distributed to people in the crowd; the following day, locals who'd missed out on the event paid as much as 25 cents for scorched bits of the victim's bones. Around the same time, in Maysville, Kentucky, onlookers haggled over the toes and fingers of Richard Coleman, a teenaged cook who'd been burned to death on suspicion of having killed a white woman. "Long after most of the mob went away little children from six to ten years of age carried dried grass and kindling wood and kept the fire burning all during the afternoon," one contemporary newspaper reported. "Relic-hunters visited the scene and carried away pieces of flesh and the negro's teeth."

Even in the north, as late as the Depression Era, souvenirs were a part of the lynching ritual. The 1930 mob-hanging of Thomas Shipp and Abram Smith in Marion, Indiana, became notorious after a now-famous photograph depicted white citizens smirking and pointing at the victims' bloodied bodies strung up on a maple tree in the courthouse square; less well known is the fact that those same citizens, eager for mementos of the event, stripped the tree of its bark in the days that followed. The photograph of the Indiana lynching was reprinted on postcards, which were sold locally and mailed to friends and family in the weeks after the event. Souvenir postcards had, in fact, been printed to commemorate lynchings since the turn of the century. "This is a token of a great day we had in Dallas," one Texan wrote on a postcard depicting the 1910 murder of a domestic laborer named Allen Brooks. "I saw this on my noon hour. I was very much in the bunch. You can see the negro on a telephone pole."

Though scholars and historians have written countless books and research papers in an attempt to make sense of the lynching epidemic that seized early twentieth-century America, few of these studies analyze the gruesome souvenir rituals that accompanied the killings. One notable exception is "The Black Body as Souvenir in American Lynching," a 2005 paper by cultural historian Harvey Young, who asserts that lynching mementos were inseparable from the mob-terror theatrics that defined the act. "The body part recalls and remembers the performance of which it is a part," he writes. "It not only gestures toward the beliefs that motivated its theft, but also renders visible the body from which it was taken." Young goes on to point out that while mob killings were by definition a public spectacle, they were ultimately enforced by the participants' after-the-fact public silence (which frustrated federal investigators, and yielded few convictions). Lynching souvenirs were not just a way to dehumanize the victim and certify the savage emotional energy of the event; they were a physical token of the unspoken assumptions that underpinned white supremacy.

Appalling as the lynching spectacle was in early twentieth-century America, collecting souvenirs from public executions had long been common in many parts of the world—particularly in Europe, where the tanned skin of hanged prisoners was sold on the street in early mid-nineteenth-century England. Execution souvenirs were so common during this era that an English hangman named George "Throttler" Smith made a small fortune by selling lengths of rope from the hanging of serial killer William Palmer in 1856. Contemporary newspapers excoriated Smith not for the amorality of his enterprise, but for rumors that some of the rope on offer had not been used in Palmer's execution.

In her essay collection *On Longing: Narratives of the Miniature, the Gigantic, the Souvenir, the Collection*, literary critic Susan Stewart characterizes the mementos of death as "anti-souvenirs":

> They mark the horrible transformation of meaning into materiality more than they mark, as other souvenirs do, the transformation of materiality into meaning. If the function of the souvenir proper is to create a continuous and personal narrative of the past, the function of such souvenirs of death is to disrupt and disclaim that continuity. Souvenirs of the mortal body are not so much a nostalgic celebration of the past as they are an erasure of the significance of history.

One death-object Stewart mentions in the context of anti-souvenirs is the human scalp, which has been used as a macabre battle trophy since the earliest recorded days of warfare (Herodotus, for example, details the ancient Scythian technique of using enemy scalps to decorate horse bridles). Though the act of mutilating enemy dead evokes images of premodern combat at the hands of Bornean warriors, barbarian Huns, or pre-Confucian Chinese bandits, the act of cutting fleshly souvenirs from dead enemies has been reported in all eras of American warfare. In the Pacific theater of the Second World War, for example, both Japanese and American troops were known to have mutilated corpses. As early as September 1942, US Pacific Fleet commanders ordered that "no part of the enemy's body may be used as a souvenir," though it was not uncommon for GIs to collect ears and teeth from dead Japanese in the wake of brutal island battles. On May 22, 1944, *LIFE Magazine*'s Picture of the Week depicted a 20-year-old Arizona woman gazing at a human skull that her Navy-lieutenant boyfriend had mailed her from New Guinea. "This is a good Jap," his accompanying note had read. "A dead one."

Negative publicity from the *LIFE* article compelled military officials to reassert their policy against taking body parts on the battlefield; a June 1944 memorandum from the US Judge Advocate General's Corps instructed officers to "take measures to search for the [enemy] wounded and dead, and to protect them against pillage and maltreatment." Official policies notwithstanding, however, the problem continued to reassert itself in subsequent American conflicts. In 2011, for instance, a US Army staff sergeant court-martialed for the "thrill-kill" murders of three Afghan civilians readily admitted to taking human fingers as souvenirs, even as he denied that his victims were noncombatants. "That was the finger he tried to kill me with," he told a military court in an attempt to justify his mutilation of a dead Afghan in Kandahar Province. "I compare it to keeping antlers off a deer I shot."

*

I should point out here that such grotesque anti-souvenirs bear little experiential resemblance to the travel keepsakes I'm examining in these pages. Unlike the innocuous mementos collected on a personal journey, death souvenirs aren't meant to be kept and enshrined over the long term. In the moment, a finger severed from an enemy corpse might speak to the kill-or-be-killed psychopathy of combat, just like a charred bit of ulna plucked from a lynching pyre certifies the triumph of racially motivated mob-rule over the prescribed impartiality of civic justice. Once the energy of such events subsides, these anti-souvenirs are, in most cases, quietly discarded.

While anti-souvenirs don't serve the same function as the keepsakes of travel, however, they do hint at the complex narratives that underpin all souvenirs. The objects collected in Enlightenment-era *Wunderkammern* represented Europe's thirst for knowledge and understanding, for example, but they also bore witness to the imperial conquest and plunder that enabled the acquisition of those objects in the first place. Similarly, the exotic souvenirs that later found their way into public institutions like the British Museum were meant to evoke the essence of distant and ancient peoples—yet as often as not those objects reduced such cultures to simplistic and demeaning stereotypes. Elsewhere, in the United States, the late-nineteenth-century vogue for collecting and curating Plains Indian artifacts coincided with brutal military campaigns that aimed to disenfranchise and subjugate those very Native American populations.

At times the acquisition of a given souvenir in a given location reinforces a narrative that sanitizes the broader realities of that place. For generations, visitors to Mount Vernon in Virginia could visit its gift shop and buy replica porcelain plates and white oak bottle-stoppers similar to what George and Martha Washington might have used in 1798. What these items failed to evoke was the fact that, in 1798, the majority of Mount Vernon's inhabitants were black slaves. Indeed, if the Washingtons enjoyed white oak furnishings in 1798, it was because wood had been harvested and crafted by men who were subject to whippings and beatings; when the First Couple ate off of fine porcelain, the food was served by women whose children could be sold off like livestock. In 1929 the Mount Vernon Ladies' Association erected a small marble monument honoring the "Faithful Colored Servants of the Washington Family," but the estate didn't offer a comprehensive depiction of slave life until 2016. The gift shop currently sells jewelry, coffee mugs, letter openers, Christmas ornaments, ballpoint pens, and vintage playing cards—but nothing to commemorate the 317 enslaved humans who labored there.

The inherent conundrum for historical tourist sites like Mount Vernon is that alluding to human suffering in the form of gift-shop souvenirs is a tricky prospect. In 1974, some thirty years after Poland's Auschwitz concentration camp was liberated by Allied troops, the New York Times published a scathing assessment of the site's "souvenir stands, Pepsi-Cola signs and the tourist-attraction atmosphere."

Auschwitz lapel pins, the article noted, were on offer, as were ballpoint pens that depicted pictures of gas chambers and crematoria. "All that seems to be lacking," one observer complained, "is a stand selling souvenir bones and ashes." In time the Auschwitz-Birkenau Memorial reduced its gift-shop offerings to a selection of books—but this in itself led to an uptick in visitors stealing away with found items such as railway spikes and bits of barbed wire. In 2014 tourist vandalism at the site got so bad that there were calls to install on-site CCTV systems—a plan Poland's culture ministry rejected as tasteless. "How would you feel if you visited Auschwitz-Birkenau barracks and noticed that there were two cameras monitoring every item?" one official told the *Daily Telegraph*. "How would we be able to maintain the [solemn atmosphere] of the camp?"

New York's National September 11 Memorial & Museum faced a similar souvenir conundrum when it opened in 2014. Since the museum doesn't receive federal funding, part of its $60-million-a-year operating budget is financed by selling 9/11-themed keepsakes such as magnets, key chains, stuffed animals, tote bags, baseballs, umbrellas, and, according to one news report, "a cheese plate shaped like a map of the US, with the three sites of the plane crashes marked on it." Such gift-shop souvenirs did not go over well with some families of 9/11 victims. "To me, it's the crassest, most insensitive thing to have a commercial enterprise at the place where my son died," one mother told the *New York Post*. "To sell baubles I find quite shocking and repugnant."

New York-based design artist Constantin Boym explored the inherent awkwardness of tragedy souvenirs with a series of miniature building replicas that he began to design and sell in 1997. Depicting historically symbolic structures such as the Texas School Book Depository, the Oklahoma City Federal Building, and Osama Bin Laden's Abbottabad safe house, Boym's "Buildings of Disaster" series was meant to push back against the notion that souvenirs are too kitschy to commemorate serious events. "In our media-saturated time, the world disasters stand as people's measure of history," Boym wrote. "The images of burning or exploded buildings make a different, populist history of architecture, one based on emotional involvement rather than on scholarly appreciation." When asked for his opinion about the items on offer in the September 11 Memorial gift shop, Boym argued that disaster souvenirs are only tacky when (as in the case of cheese plates and umbrellas) their symbolism gets mixed up with trivial uses. "9/11 memorial merchandise should be devoid of all unrelated functionalism," he said. "The souvenir [should be] a psychological 'container,' where the users could put their own personal memories and emotions."

*

Similar ethical challenges present themselves in environments where tourist gift shops don't exist. In April of 2006, the military newspaper *Stars and Stripes* published an article outlining which souvenir items were and were not permissible for US troops to bring home from Iraq. According to Camp

Anaconda's judge advocate, service members could keep legally purchased or captured military items such as helmets, uniforms, flags, canteens, nonretractable bayonets, training manuals, and Saddam Hussein-era currency. Soldiers were not, however, allowed to bring home grenades, firearms, switchblades, personal items taken from the enemy, sand, dirt, rocks, plants, animals, and any scientific, archaeological, religious, or historical artifacts.

Though the article didn't state it explicitly, part of the reason military officials were clarifying war-souvenir protocols was that Iraqi contraband had begun showing up on internet auction sites such as eBay. Items purportedly seized from Saddam Hussein's palaces—oriental rugs, gilt-embossed Korans, ceremonial swords—were hot sellers, as was silverware bearing the Iraqi Army crest. More unsettling for US military officials hoping to stay on good terms with their host country were items of historical and archaeological import, such as antique coins and alabaster cylinder seals. One officer quoted in the article had ominous words for soldiers taking such items out of the country illegally. "It will prolong your stay here," he said, "and shorten your career."

Stern words notwithstanding, the *Stars and Stripes* article revealed something time-honored and traditional about war souvenirs, even as the rise of online retailing (and the corresponding transparency with which war contraband was being resold) suggested that something new was happening. Indeed, while the anti-souvenir ritual of mutilating enemy dead has come to be seen as a troublesome anomaly in modern warfare, bringing found and scavenged objects home from battle zones remains so common as to be universal among rank-and-file soldiers. Issuing official guidelines about which items make safe and acceptable war souvenirs goes back at least to the First World War, when battle-weary doughboys risked life and limb to collect war detritus and fashion it into "trench art" (shrapnel-fragment letter openers, artillery-shell flower vases, etc.) that they could take home when the war ended.

Unlike tourist mementos, which have come to reflect a wide array of individualized meanings as travel has become more accessible, battle-zone souvenirs serve a more specific emotional narrative—one that is difficult for people who haven't experienced war to understand. In his philosophical memoir *The Warriors: Reflections on Men in Battle*, Second World War veteran Jesse Glenn Gray attempted to explain the psychology that drives this behavior:

> Much of the American soldier's passion for souvenirs in recent wars may have stemmed not so much from a primitive desire to loot or even from the desire to establish in postwar memory his claim "to having been there," though both these motives were undoubtedly present in some degree. Primarily, souvenirs appeared to give the soldier some assurance of his future beyond the destructive environment of the present. They represented a promise that he might survive.

Gray goes on to explain how war mementos serve as psychic talismans for soldiers who might otherwise feel "unbearably exposed and vulnerable" in circumstances over which they have little control. "Perhaps all of us," he adds, "in peace or in war, use possessions for a similar purpose, as a defense against the world."

West African Edo saltcellar, Kingdom of Benin, 16th century

7 SOUVENIRS AND (THE COMPLICATED NOTION OF) AUTHENTICITY

Though anti-souvenirs are a category separate from the keepsakes of travel, death mementos do occasionally make their way into the tourist market. In the early twentieth century, for example, adventure travelers to South America were known to collect shrunken human heads made by the Amazonian Shuar tribe. Known locally as *tsantsa*, these macabre ceremonial objects took weeks to make, and were the result of the Shuar's ongoing conflict with the Achuar, a rival Jivaroan tribe living in the Marañon River basin of northern Peru and eastern Ecuador. When a series of museum exhibitions and magazine articles sparked American and European interest in *tsantsa* at the end of the nineteenth century, shrunken heads began to appear in curio shops from Peru to Panama. By the 1930s, specialist vendors in South America were hawking *tsantsa* to tourists for twenty-five dollars per shrunken head, and the Peruvian and Ecuadorian governments were struggling to stem the trade.

Years later, long after the practice of buying and importing shrunken heads had been outlawed, American researchers determined that most of the presumed *tsantsa* owned by museums and collectors were fake. What seemed to be a withered and wrinkled human visage was, in most cases, a monkey's head, a sloth's head, or cured goatskin that had been artfully molded, textured, and shaved into passably anthropomorphic form. Moreover, many of the *tsantsa* made from actual human skin hadn't come from the Shuar, but from morgue-raiding taxidermists in places like Bogota and Panama City. In a 1937 report for the Smithsonian's Bureau of American Ethnology, scientist Matthew Stirling noted that "the majority of heads which leave the country were never in the hands of the [Shuar] but were prepared by various individuals from the bodies of unclaimed paupers to supply the constant demand of tourists and travelers." A final irony of the *tsantsa* trade, Stirling noted, was that the tourist demand for shrunken heads had altered the Shuar ritual of collecting them: in addition to killing their enemies over localized conflicts, the Shuar—having learned that *tsantsa* could be traded for manufactured goods such as shotguns— began to harvest Achuar heads for commercial purposes.

In a sense, the early twentieth-century trade in bogus *tsantsa* was part of a time-honored tradition of souvenir fakery. As we have seen, medieval pilgrims venerated dubiously sourced saints' bones, Renaissance-era *Wunderkammern* displayed sham dragon wings, Grand Tourists collected recently forged shards of "ancient pottery," and Thomas Jefferson cut chips from a chair that had probably never come into contact with William Shakespeare's rear end. What had changed by the twentieth century, however, was that the expansion of global manufacturing and commerce had fueled an intensified interest in the very concept of authenticity. As travel became easier and gift shops the world over offered an increasingly standardized selection of factory-made knickknacks, discerning travelers sought to validate their experiences by seeking souvenirs rooted in local traditions and exotic practices.

This was, in fact, part of a much broader conversation about finding meaning in the modern world. Philosopher Walter Benjamin, writing about urbanism in the 1920s, used two different German words for "experience"—*erfahrung* and *erlebnis*—to examine how modernity had affected the ways we interact with our surroundings. *Erfahrung*, he suggested, was rooted in an ethos of tradition and practiced knowledge, whereas *erlebnis* was a more reactive shock response to an ever-changing, over-stimulated world. Though Benjamin never extended the analogy to include travel souvenirs, one could readily conclude that collectable teaspoons and picture postcards were emblematic of a superficial *erlebnis* travel experience, whereas tribal jewelry and ritual handicrafts (or, in extreme cases, Shuar *tsantsa* heads) were meant to signify a more genuine *erfahrung* encounter with other places. Folk objects, in other words, were thought to exude an existential authenticity that mass-produced objects did not.

The problem, of course, was that the modern concept of authenticity invariably got mixed up with exoticized notions of how faraway cultures lived. This naturally applied to the colonial-era fixation with Shuar headhunters and other societies deemed primitive or "savage"—but as the twentieth century progressed it also attached itself to any faraway culture that felt rooted in a traditional past. "Paradoxically, the search [for authenticity] is itself an expression of the modernity from which the tourist seeks to escape," anthropologist Erve Chambers noted in his book *Native Tours*. "In this sense, the attachment of the label *traditional* to particular objects, places, and people serves to establish the pervasive influence of modernity by imagining those few objects of desire that are supposedly not modern." As often as not, this meant that the modern traveler's imaginative sense for authenticity blurred into simplistic stereotypes. Usually these premodern fantasies were projected onto non-Western cultures, but not always. After a fruitless 1953 location-scouting trip for the movie *Brigadoon*, for example, the movie producer Arthur Freed expressed disappointment with the villages he'd seen in the Scottish Highlands, quipping, "I went to Scotland but I could find nothing that looked like Scotland."

Stereotyped expectations on the part of modern tourists evolved in tandem with the rise of photography, which began to influence people's perceptions of what distant places were supposed to look like. When Japan began to industrialize in the latter decades of the nineteenth century, for instance, Western travelers looking to commemorate their visit to the island were less interested in the complexities of a modernizing society than idealized fantasies of a bygone feudal culture. Photo studios in cities like Tokyo thus learned to adapt to the desires of Europeans and Americans, selling tourists pictures of models dressed as samurais and geishas, even as their Japanese clients sat for photos wearing frock coats and top hats. This disconnect between documentary reality and sentimental projection only intensified as mass media expanded (and tourist snapshot-cameras became ubiquitous) in the twentieth century. In his acerbic 1962 book *The Image*, historian Daniel J. Boorstin compared foreign countries to celebrities, noting that tourists had come to evaluate places not by using reality to make sense of their media-driven expectations, but by using media-driven expectations to make sense of reality. "The tourist seldom likes the authentic (to him often unintelligible) product of the foreign culture; he prefers his own provincial expectations," Boorstin wrote. "The French chanteuse singing English with a French accent seems more charmingly French than one who simply sings in French. The American tourist in Japan looks less for what is Japanese than what is Japanesey."

As often as not, travelers' expectations had economic stakes, and local communities that grew to rely on the tourist trade wound up "performing" semi-fictional versions of their own cultures. By the mid-twentieth century the Native

American souvenirs on offer in the Southwestern United States owed as much to Hollywood Westerns as to Hopi or Navajo traditions, and the markets of Baghdad and Teheran sold "oriental" knickknacks—gaudy amulets and astrolabes embossed with zodiac signs—that reflected *Arabian Nights* fantasies more than local handicraft practices. Even in isolated communities where few media expectations existed, tourists tended to see native cultures in terms of premodern caricature. When Ethiopia's Omo Valley opened up to tourists toward the end of the twentieth century, for example, tribes like the Mursi and the Hamar discovered that charging a fee to have their pictures taken was a great source of hard currency. As these tribes invested the extra cash into modern comforts, however, they soon discovered a paradox at the heart of their endeavor: tourists, it turned out, wouldn't pay money for snapshots of Mursi or Hamar tribesmen clutching transistor radios and wearing T-shirts; they wanted pictures of primitive-looking people clutching spears and wearing goat skins. In time, economic necessity compelled these tribespeople to hide their blue jeans and don their most ostentatious war paint and loincloths whenever they saw tour buses approaching.

Western anthropologists and sociologists—who by the 1970s had discovered that tourist behavior could be as puzzling and worthy of empirical study as indigenous behavior—began to call this expectation-driven feedback loop "staged authenticity." Despite the complex realities of an ever-changing world, it seemed, travelers from industrialized countries preferred to view local cultures through a profoundly conservative, tradition-obsessed lens. As modern tourists sought out hypothetical ideals of purity in Finnish Laplanders and Panamanian Kuna, local cultures learned to cash in by presenting more stereotypical versions of themselves. When Laplanders and Kuna sang songs and sold handicrafts that reflected their premodern pasts, they weren't really telling their own stories; they were filling in the blanks of idealized narratives that, essentially, belonged to the tourists.

*

Over the years anthropologists and museum curators have developed all manner of objective methods—from ethnological analysis to carbon dating—to help determine which cultural artifacts are and are not authentic. Tourists face a more ambiguous task in determining authenticity, in part because the very process of shopping for souvenirs has a way of muddling the concept.

I first began to grasp this while traveling in India in 2001. Not wanting to settle for the gift-shop tchotchkes on offer in my hotel, I took a series of buses to Calcutta's old colonial-era Hogg Market to look for something more authentically representative of India. As it turned out, the Hogg Market offered a wealth of pan-Indian souvenir items—from Keralan Kathakali masks, to Jaipuri *razai* quilts, to Punjabi *jutti* slippers—but most of them were sold in a cluster of stalls that clearly catered to tourists. While Germans and Canadians marveled at *dhurrie* carpets and Kashmiri silks, actual Calcutta Indians flocked to other quarters of the bazaar, where they haggled over rubber bathmats, stainless steel cooking pans, and polyester brocade fabric. To all appearances the Kathputli puppets the stall-vendors proffered to me were culturally accurate, but the fact that they had been manufactured for the souvenir trade (rather than Rajasthani performances) made me wonder if they were really as authentic as they seemed.

As it happens, ethnologists and curators have typically sought to enforce that very distinction, asserting that objects created for and sold to tourists are culturally inferior, even when made by the same craftsmen (using the same materials) as traditional ritual or functional objects. By this standard, a locally crafted terra-cotta jug is authentic when it's made to carry water through a village, but inauthentic when it's made for some distant tourist market. Similarly, a handcrafted religious totem is a sacred object when placed on a remote tribal altar, but "tourist art" when placed on a gift-shop display shelf. Utility and context are thus thought to determine authenticity, even among objects of identical construction and appearance.

The problem with this distinction is its presumption that authenticity lies in cultural self-containment rather than cultural interaction and adaptation. The passage of time is also a factor. The British Museum, for example, would probably never display Indian Kathputli puppets that had been fashioned to resemble Manchester United football players, but it does exhibit a sixteenth-century African-ivory saltcellar that had been carved to depict Europeans with long hair, beards, and hooked noses. This saltcellar, which was created by artisans in the Kingdom of Benin and sold to Portuguese traders, was in effect a tainted object, since carved-ivory art had traditionally been made to honor the Edo king's ancestors. By the rigid standards of objective authenticity, these saltcellars were a degradation of Benin Edo art customs—but with five hundred years of hindsight, these objects have come to emblematize the historical trade partnership between a powerful African kingdom and its imperial European counterpart.

In the modern era, tourism and cross-cultural commerce have transformed ethnic art traditions in most all corners of the world. In Papua New Guinea's Sepik River basin, for example, local craftsmen have, over time, altered their woodcarving traditions to appeal to tourists' tastes and expectations. For the most part, these Papuan artists consider this practice separate from their private ceremonial artwork, and—like pragmatic merchants the world over—they have adapted their techniques to create masks, flutes, and figurines that appeal to specific market demands, continuing (or discontinuing) designs based upon how well they sell. The result is a dynamic and ever-changing style of art that has blurred the line between local and global. It has also made isolated Papuan communities more economically sustainable. "Many people in the middle Sepik remain in villages rather than migrating to urban centers precisely because tourism ensures a steady source of cash," anthropologist Eric Silverman reported in the 1990s, noting that villages frequented by souvenir-hunting tourists had come to be considered wealthy, and attracted all manner of new trade with more isolated Papuan settlements. In this sense, the modern souvenir trade didn't degrade Sepik Papuan identity so much as reinforce it.

Elsewhere in the world, the creation and sale of tourist souvenirs has been a way to assert ethnic identity and economic opportunity in areas where outside forces have destroyed traditional ways of life. In Brazil, Pataxó tribespeople displaced from their ancestral hunting homelands by cattle ranchers and cacao farmers turned to selling ethnic handicrafts as a way to maintain a living. Everyday Pataxó objects like bracelets and drinking bowls became more ornate and colorful to cater to tourist tastes, and before long tribal craftspeople began to apply indigenous designs to nonindigenous items like hats, earrings, and hairpins. In this way, Pataxó material culture managed to proliferate and transform, even as its traditional homeland was lost to corporate agriculture interests.

Perhaps the most well-documented transformation of local folkcrafts happened when the island of Bali began to modernize in the mid–late twentieth century. As tourists flocked to the island for its scenic beaches and distinctive Hindu cultural traditions, Bali's carvers, musicians, and dancers reinvigorated ancient art traditions as a way to earn cash for things like motorcycles and television sets (which were discreetly hidden away when tourists arrived in the village). Most visitors were content to buy traditional Balinese carvings, but as more and more mass tourists arrived at art-mecca villages like Ubud, craftsmen began to fulfill requests to carve wooden souvenirs of such non-Balinese deities as *Tintin*, King Tut, and *Pinocchio*. Some tourists complained as more and more pop-culture-themed carvings began to appear in the Ubud Traditional Art Market, but the Balinese artists themselves were unfazed. "Interviews with producers and sellers of these products reveal that the craft of woodcutting as such is what the Balinese are good at and have done for many centuries," noted tourism-management scholar Frans Schouten. "Such an attitude makes clear that the act of sculpting is considered more essential for the cultural identity of the Balinese than the forms that are created in the act." Schouten goes on to note that representational art at events like the Balinese New Year Festival has evolved in tandem with the times:

Traditionally effigies in the form of huge monsters are made in every village and neighborhood to drive out the evil spirits from the island. There is a traditional design for these monsters, but increasingly other images are used as well to frighten the spirits. We noticed enormous Hells Angels on motorbikes and tourists depicted as drunkards with a beer bottle. Some view these as derivations of the original design, but one can also perceive them as proof of the vitality of the underlying belief system that uses new images of what locally is considered to be horror, to frighten off the evil spirits even more effectively.

If the adaptability of Balinese artists has given rise to an authenticity problem, it's less likely to exist on the island itself than in places affected by the reach of globalized import-export markets. In Australia, for example, Aboriginal craftspeople have, since the 1970s, been able to make a good living creating souvenir boomerangs, didgeridoos, and dot paintings that reflect indigenous traditions. Since Australia has a higher cost of living than surrounding Asian-Pacific nations, however, a deluge of cheap "Aboriginal-style" knockoff souvenirs made in Bali, Vietnam, and China have in recent years undercut the price of Aboriginal art. "It really pains me to see [an imported] boomerang or didgeridoo," one Aboriginal gallery owner admitted in a 2016 Australian TV interview. "Did you know those Bali didgeridoos are made out of bamboo? It's cringe-worthy. It doesn't have anything to do with our culture."

*

In a certain sense, seeking authenticity in a given travel souvenir isn't about the object itself so much as the traveler's sense of self-identity. In Western societies, where we nitpick the difference between "tourists" and "travelers," collecting authentic-seeming souvenirs can be a way of convincing ourselves—and, just as importantly, convincing others—that we have somehow grasped the behind-the-scenes essence of a place and its inhabitants. It is, in short, a status ritual—and rituals of status have more to do with the social expectations of our home cultures than the cultures we visit.

To better understand how identifying (and signifying) authenticity in travel settings is a peculiarly Western concern, it's useful to look at the tourist habits of a non-Western culture such as Japan, where the word for souvenir (お土産, or *omiyage*) carries a different set of assumptions. Unlike in Europe or the United States, where souvenir acquisition is a matter of individualized taste, the Japanese tradition of buying *omiyage* is tied to a delicate network of social obligations back home. Though some Japanese travelers do buy keepsakes for themselves, the formal *omiyage* ritual focuses on acquiring gifts for family, friends, and coworkers. These gifts are less an act of personal thoughtfulness than an obligatory gesture of respect and apology for the traveler's absence from domestic duties. Literally translated, *omiyage* means "local product" (土 = "soil," 産 = "production"), and journeys to different parts of Japan carry a standardized set of souvenir expectations, usually centered on food. A traveler to Kyoto might be expected to bring home green-tea-flavored sweets, whereas a trip to Aomori obligates the purchase of apple-flavored pastries. Since appearance is an important part of gift-giving rituals in Japan, colorful boxes of prewrapped *omiyage* are invariably stocked at local department stores and train stations.

Train transportation was, as it happened, a key component in the evolution of the *omiyage* ritual, since food-based souvenirs didn't keep well in the days before modern conveyance. In Japan's preindustrial Edo Period, Shinto pilgrims brought home small charms and *sake* cups that evoked the blessings of the shrine and certified the journey. As the nation modernized during the nineteenth-century Meiji Restoration, *omiyage* emerged as a more secular way to commemorate travel, celebrate the country's abundance, and honor social obligations. At first *omiyage* were purchased primarily for people who'd given the traveler *senbetsu*—that is, departing gifts, usually cash or supplies for the journey. In time *omiyage* were brought home and distributed to friends and family independently of *senbetsu*, though reciprocal obligations remained important. Oftentimes *omiyage* were purchased to honor a person who'd gifted *omiyage* after a previous journey—and great care was taken to ensure the new souvenir wasn't too cheap or too expensive to upset the social balance.

The *omiyage*-acquisition ritual got more complicated when overseas business and leisure travel became commonplace for Japanese citizens in the 1970s and 1980s. Whereas travelers leaving a given city within Japan could choose from a wide selection of gift-wrapped items right there in the train station, buying souvenirs in other countries presented a more time-consuming shopping task. Since *omiyage* obligations could extend to dozens of people back home, Japanese tourists were often compelled to curtail sightseeing excursions and cut back on dining expenses to free up enough time and money to fulfill their souvenir commitments. Eventually, as the Japanese travel market expanded overseas, department stores in much-visited cities like Paris began to package local products in the manner of *omiyage*. By the 1990s vendors in Tokyo's Narita Airport had simplified the process by offering iconic international souvenirs (French perfume, Swiss chocolates, Scottish whiskey, Hawaiian macadamia nuts) to Japanese travelers arriving home from those very destinations. These days, Japanese travelers who don't have the time or desire for extensive souvenir-shopping sprees in other countries can order home-delivered *omiyage* from specialized websites.

By certain standards of authenticity, commemorating a trip to Europe by purchasing Swiss chocolates in a Japanese airport rings a bit absurd. According to the protocols of *omiyage*, however, the souvenir object itself is purely symbolic; its authenticity derives from the preestablished social relationship between the giver and receiver. This same dynamic can apply, if in a less ritualized way, when Western tourists buy their own travel gifts for friends and family.

But even a Western tourist who collects souvenirs for private, individualistic ends is engaging in an authenticity ritual that isn't really about the object itself. Even when the souvenir in question lives up to museum-level criteria of anthropological purity, the item's objective authenticity is, in actual practice, subordinate to the authenticity the traveler *feels* upon acquiring it. And, ironically, this subjective feeling applies as readily to a mass-produced Eiffel Tower key chain as to a bona fide Shuar *tsantsa* head. Status considerations aside, experience doesn't authenticate the souvenir; the souvenir authenticates experience.

Indeed, the process of collecting personal souvenirs invariably serves what sociologist Ning Wang calls "existential authenticity"—a sense that the object reflects a more genuine sense of selfhood in the person who acquired it. "Tourists are not merely searching for authenticity of the *Other*," Wang notes. "They also search for the authenticity of, and between, *themselves*. . . . In such a liminal experience, people feel they themselves are much more authentic and more freely self-expressed than in everyday life, not because they find the toured objects are authentic but simply because they are engaging in non-ordinary activities, free from the constraints of the daily."

Existential authenticity is underscored by the fact that, as travelers, we are by definition itinerant outsiders—strangers in strange lands—who don't possess the experience or knowledge to objectively evaluate the things we see along the way. When we collect souvenirs, we do so not to evaluate the world, but to narrate the self.

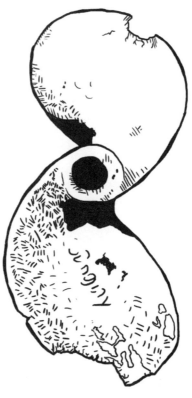

Laotian riverboat propeller, author's collection, 1999

8 SOUVENIRS, MEMORY, AND THE SHORTNESS OF LIFE

My Mongolian *Tsaghan Ebügen* mask, with its wispy white beard and mad-eyed old-man grin, now hangs on a wall near a bookshelf in my office. I can see it as I type this. Nailed beneath it are my Korean, Chinese, Filipino, and Balinese masks, as well as a Greek-theater mask that I brought home from Athens to fill space on the wall after my Japanese *Gigaku* mask fell off the wall and broke during home renovations. The other end of my bookshelf features a row of Burmese *yoke thé* marionette heads beneath a dented aluminum riverboat propeller that I kept after traveling down the Laotian Mekong in 1999.

Taken together, these souvenirs represent the seven years I spent living and traveling in Asia in the late 1990s and early 2000s (even the Greek mask, acquired in Europe in 2006, takes me back to that Asia-centric time of my life). Taken individually, however, these items don't exactly evoke distinctive memories from the moment of their acquisition. For the most part, these masks remind me of gift shops and market stalls in places like Seoul, Beijing, and Cebu. Only the Laotian riverboat propeller, perched anomalously among the marionette heads, came into my possession via a non-shopping experience—specifically, a thrilling, dangerous, and faintly harebrained adventure that involved buying a Mekong fishing boat with two other Americans and driving it 900 miles from Luang Prabang to the Cambodian border. (The divots in the propeller are a telling detail, since, in our early naïveté, we smashed upward of a dozen cheap aluminum rotors on rocky Mekong shoals before wising up and buying a steel one.)

Of the masks themselves, the Mongolian *Tsaghan Ebügen* evokes the strongest travel associations for me—not for what it represents culturally, but because the act of buying it in Ulaanbaatar back in 2001 made me reconsider the very meaning of the souvenir ritual. Indeed, for all of the collective and historical ends that travel keepsakes have served over the past 4,000 years, the private acquisition of a souvenir rarely represents a simple, one-to-one token of a place or experience. Future memories aside, buying souvenirs is often something the traveler does as a matter of routine in a strange land, kind of like sightseeing or trying out local food. "Tourists, who are away from their normal environment, possibly even in very different environments, need something familiar," writes tourism-retail scholar Kirsten K. Swanson. "Shopping provides a sense of comfort and homelike stability. Souvenirs are the prop, or the excuse, for participating in this 'ordinary activity' in an unordinary environment." Oftentimes this comfort-ritual takes the form of buying gifts for loved ones—a way of reflecting on relationships with family and friends at a time when one is far from home and surrounded by strangers.

Even when travel keepsakes are found or kept objects, collecting souvenirs can be a way of slowing down a real-time experience that is by definition ephemeral. A journey to a faraway place can be disorienting (even as it is vivid and stimulating), and the tourist thus collects mementos as a way of gaining power over moments that he doesn't fully understand—the speed and efficiency of modern travel plays into this. As anthropologist Nelson H. H. Graburn has noted, jet-age technologies "diminish experienced reality, and the mementos and souvenirs serve as cues by which to relive the experience at a slower pace." This often goes hand in hand with the desire to make a distant experience seem real once one has returned home. Much like an autograph from a celebrity, the souvenir ratifies that the encounter (however fleeting it was) really happened. In this way, souvenirs can be a mechanism of reflection and wonder—a concrete way of reminding its owner that, once upon a time, she had experiences in a faraway place.

The fact that I have, in these pages, referred to my Asian masks by native terms like *Tsaghan Ebügen* and *Nojang* (rather than simply describing them by appearance) hints at another, more performative dynamic that underpins souvenirs. Indeed, souvenirs don't just allude to a journey or a destination; they oftentimes seek to advertise the worldliness of the traveler who collected them. Much like Renaissance-era nobles used *Wunderkammern* to showcase knowledge and erudition, travel souvenirs can thus serve as a kind of exotic status symbol—proof that the owner has gone someplace most people haven't and gained knowledge that most people don't possess. This souvenir status ritual has diminished a bit in recent years, as travelers can more readily showcase their far-flung achievements on social media—but it has always hinted at the ways the significance of a given travel memento invariably involves after-the-fact embellishment on the part of its owner. As I noted before, I never witnessed these masks onstage in actual Mongolian or Korean drama performances—and in fact I didn't even remember the terms *Tsaghan Ebügen* or *Nojang* until I looked them up using Google image search while researching this book.

By certain standards of postcolonial analysis, the fact that I chose to commemorate my time in Mongolia and Korea with archaic-looking shamanist performance masks might well betray a souvenir version of "othering"—that is, viewing other cultures purely in terms of stereotypical and seemingly exotic differences. In Korea in particular, where I spent two years teaching English to tech-savvy middle-class college students, a more appropriate souvenir might well have been a cassette tape of, say, the mid-1990s dance-pop/ metal fusion band Seo Taiji and Boys, or an empty bottle of Jinro *soju*. In spite of the ways I encountered a rapidly modernizing Korean culture on a day-to-day level, however, I was somehow compelled to buy a souvenir that spoke to stereotypical shorthand rather than lived experience. Interestingly enough, my Korean students did the same thing when they vacationed in the United States—favoring cowboy knickknacks and James Dean kitsch over more authentically representative mementos of 1990s America. For Koreans as much as Americans, souvenirs served to authenticate a pretravel vision of the Other as much as they did the journey itself.

This compulsion to collect shorthand symbols of our own expectations in faraway places is why Eiffel Tower kitsch sells so well in Paris, and why tourists seek out traditional handicrafts in the same shopping districts where local people opt for simpler-to-use manufactured goods. Some types of souvenirs have become globally popular simply because they evoke a vaguely exotic notion of the Other. According to Kirsten Swanson, "carved masks can be bought in almost all less developed countries, even in places where carved masks were never used in rituals, celebrations, or battles. Tourists like carved masks, so destination residents produce them for profit." Tourism scholar Frans Schouten adds that dimly grasped notions of Otherness have created "a kind of universal stock for souvenir retail," even industrialized parts of the world like Europe:

Pictures of girls taking a bath in a pond are for sale everywhere, as well as portraits of children with a teardrop. And no one has been able to give me a reasonable explanation for the occurrence of sets of Japanese samurai swords in many souvenir shops all over Europe. Equally universally for sale are "dream catchers," based upon a design that originates from Native American tribes. They are available all over the world, from Ireland to Bali. Their popularity remains so far unexplained but one could argue that they have become the very icons of the "otherness" of a visited place. It is interesting in this respect that the "otherness" is emphasized with objects that are iconic for a feeling, not for the place itself. The dream catcher as an omnipresent souvenir confirms in a way that tourism is dreamtime.

Though all these concepts were in play when I bought my *Tsaghan Ebügen* mask in Mongolia, however, my real epiphany didn't center on status rituals, projections of Otherness, the comfortable familiarity of shopping, or the desire to slow down time. What I realized in Ulaanbaatar was that my compulsion to buy souvenir masks was tied to long-held travel aspirations I'd first felt while hanging out with my American friend Brian, who'd taught English with me in Korea. Brian was, at the time, a more experienced traveler than I, and he'd festooned his Pusan apartment with ornate masks from places like Indonesia, Japan, and China. Nearly every weekend during my first year in Korea,

Brian and I would drink Cass Lager at his flat and talk about all the places in the world we wanted to visit. Brian never directly suggested that I should buy masks, but looking at his collection was one of the ways I dreamed about my own Asian travels in the days before I'd saved enough money to make them a reality.

When I finally set out to see these countries for myself, collecting masks became a way of certifying that I was finally acting on my travel dreams. Asian masks were, in a sense, objects that belonged to the person I had wanted to become; by the time I'd reached Mongolia I had been traveling long enough that shopping for masks felt less important. Now, when I see the *Tsaghan Ebügen* grinning on my office wall, it reminds me of that earlier version of myself, a person who used masks as a way of dreaming himself into a journey, and then—once that journey was properly underway—realized he no longer needed to keep collecting them.

*

Walk through my house, and you might not pay particular attention to the Asian masks flanking my office bookshelf; they are just a few of the many keepsakes I've chosen to collect and display over the years. Some of my souvenir objects (Ethiopian Mursi lip-plates, New Orleans Mardi Gras beads, an Australian boomerang) count as mementos of travel. Other relics I keep on my shelves (plastic fireman figurines from my childhood, a 1992-era cassette mixtape I can no longer play, my grandfather's old Zippo lighter) don't evoke distant landscapes so much as distant times of life. Some objects (a bar of soap from Manhattan's now-defunct Chelsea Hotel, a topographical map I once used to navigate the Colorado backcountry) recall previous travels and previous life-phases in equal measure. My spare room contains enough Kansas City Royals memorabilia (baseballs, beer steins, bobbleheads) to qualify as a shrine, and my informal collection of pebbles from distant shores has long since outgrown my ability to recall where most of them came from.

Most of these objects are unremarkable in and of themselves (and, in the case of pebbles and hotel soaps, they were even less remarkable in their original contexts); what gives them significance is the fact that they've ended up here together, in what amounts to a kind of collage-autobiography. Everyone who collects souvenirs ends up creating these object-narratives, which resonate with private meanings no written autobiography could ever achieve. When astronaut Neil Armstrong died in 2012, for instance, his estate executors discovered that he'd saved a few workaday items—an emergency wrench, a waist tether, a mirror—as souvenirs from his 1969 moon landing. For all that was written about the Apollo 11 mission, these simple objects suggest a story that only Armstrong could appreciate at an intuitive-emotional level.

As sophisticated as Armstrong's moon mission was, his desire to keep these items as souvenirs was rooted in a universal impulse that goes back to childhood. Nobody sits us down and tells us to collect objects when we're young; it's just something we do, as a way of familiarizing ourselves with the world, its possibilities, and our place in it. And while adults typically see souvenirs as a way of preserving lived experience, children seek and keep objects for more fundamental reasons. "The behavior of children as young as toddlers shows that possessions are not just utilitarian devices," notes scholar Stacey Menzel Baker. "In general, possessions provide the child with an emerging sense of control and self-effectance over his or her environment." As children grow older, the keepsakes they collect don't just give them a feeling of stability; they help create and interpret a sense of self. Even as adults, the private mythologies we attach to souvenirs are a way of mythologizing our own lives. Like Proustian madeleines, these objects invoke a personalized sense of the past—a universe of "lost time"—that can be felt in the present moment.

Souvenirs and similar mementos thus find their power in the way the object itself, like a broken-off chunk of bygone time, can trigger subjective reveries of distant places, people, and events. In this way souvenirs are like a similar visual keepsake, the photograph. Unlike the memories called forth by photos, however, souvenir memories are more associational, less visually specific, more unique to the object's owner, and more likely to transform over time. Often this means that the importance of a given souvenir will wax and wane—telling slightly different stories, in slightly different voices—in tandem with the self-perception and worldview of its owner. For all the importance I attached to the Chicago "seashell" I plucked from the shores of Lake Michigan at age seven, for example (and for all the years I used it to dream about onward journeys), I no longer recall what became of it. At some point in life, as I became more well-traveled and more removed from the person I was at age seven, the souvenir clamshell that meant so much to me as a kid became just another object, most likely cast aside as I moved from place to place in my twenties.

Inversely, some souvenir objects can gain meaning—often connected to greater world events—over the course of time. In 2005, for instance, I caught a string of colorful Mardi Gras beads during a Krewe of Bacchus parade in New Orleans. I was at the tail end of a three-month French Quarter sublet at the time, and I liked the retro look of the Bacchus beads, but I never figured I'd display them in my house as a souvenir of New Orleans. It wasn't until later that year—after Katrina-triggered floods had destroyed much of the city—that I took my Bacchus beads out of a storage box and displayed them on a shelf in my office. In February of 2005 that string of Bacchus beads had been little more than Mardi Gras kitsch; by September of that same year, they had come to symbolize a version of the city that no longer existed (accordingly, I was no longer just a person who'd witnessed a fairly standard New Orleans "super krewe" parade; I was a person who had witnessed history as it was about to happen). Similarly, I have, over time, come to attach sentimental meaning to travel objects that were never meant to serve as souvenirs. For all of the gift-shop souvenirs I collected during a multi-month journey across Egypt, Jordan, Syria, and Israel in my early thirties, nothing takes me back to the experience quite so effectively as the battered pair of Asolo hiking boots I wore as I walked through those landscapes. Those boots have become too worn out to use in any practical sense, but I've kept them in my closet because they evoke the Middle East more effectively than any of the Egyptian papyri or Damascus brocade displayed elsewhere in my house.

Though I've worked as a travel writer for nearly twenty years now, no story I've written is quite so personal and threaded with intuitive meaning as the ever-changing collection of souvenirs I keep in my house. Visitors might come into my home and see a boat propeller, a topographical map, or a bearded old-man mask; I look at the same objects and get an idiosyncratic glimpse into other parts of the world, other people I've known, other versions of myself. Souvenirs from distant places have helped me define the place I've come to call home, just as keepsakes from distant times have helped me define my place in the ongoing moment. And, try as I might to articulate to other people the meanings and backstories of these objects, they ultimately exist as a kind of private sign language that only I can understand.

*

Months ago, when I first started to research this book, my father's older sister, Lynda Ireland, died at age 83. Aunt Lynda was a smart, funny, feisty woman—a voracious reader who couldn't be bothered with a euphemism when a swearword would do. When I was seven years old she (along with Dale, her second husband) took me to my first Kansas City Royals game, and when I was 13 she encouraged my nascent interest in writing by slipping me Stephen King books. She and I faithfully swapped handwritten letters back in the days before email—a correspondence that stretched from Kansas to Oregon to Asia as I grew into adulthood. A few weeks after Lynda's death, her son invited me to his house to go through some boxes of my aunt's belongings, and keep whatever interested me.

By this point most all of Lynda's possessions—from kitchenware and handmade quilts to the house she'd lived in for the past three decades—had been sold off or handed down to her children and grandchildren. What was left over in the boxes were items without much practical utility or resale value—mainly photo albums, scrapbooks, and a handful of souvenirs (brass figurines, alabaster carvings, picture postcards) that her immediate family hadn't been interested in keeping. Looking at those items, I was struck by how much of what we collect in life ultimately becomes depleted of meaning: without any sense for the memories or desires that led Lynda to save these keepsakes, they felt like a sorrowful menagerie of lost objects. I ended up taking a small alabaster elephant, which I now keep perched on a coffee table in my living room.

Like all of the souvenirs I keep in my house, that alabaster elephant has come to take on multiple meanings. It is at once a reminder of my Aunt Lynda, a narrative cipher, and a memento mori—a reminder that the things we own, like life itself, can only be appreciated in real time, on ephemeral terms. I see the carved elephant as I might see a disembodied chip of wood from some faraway Stratford armchair, or fistful of dirt from a chapel floor in Jerusalem—as an object that once gave concrete meaning to experience, only to once again (and inevitably) be rendered abstract by time.

SELECTED SOURCES

"A souvenir shard from a visit to Shakespeare's house," *Monticello Newsletter*, Spring 2006.

Adams, Percy G., *Travel Literature and the Evolution of the Novel* (University Press of Kentucky, 1983).

"At Auschwitz, a Discordant Atmosphere of Tourism," *New York Times*, November 3, 1974.

Baker, Stacey Menzel, Susan Schultz Kleine, and Heather E. Bowenand, "On the Symbolic Meanings of Souvenirs for Children," *Research in Consumer Behavior*, Volume 10, 2006.

Barnhart, Robert K., *The Barnhart Dictionary of Etymology* (H. W. Wilson, 1988).

Baudrillard, Jean, *The System of Objects*, translated by James Benedict (Verso, 1996).

Benjamin, Walter, *Illuminations: Essays and Reflections*, translated by Hannah Arendt (Random House, 1968).

Benson, Tracey, "The museum of the personal: Souvenirs and nostalgia," Master's thesis, Queensland University of Technology, 2001.

Bird Jr., William L., *Souvenir Nation: Relics, Keepsakes, and Curios from the Smithsonian's National Museum of American History* (Princeton Architectural Press, 2013).

Boorstin, Daniel, *The Discoverers* (Random House, 1983).

Boorstin, Daniel, *The Image: A Guide to Pseudo-events in America* (Harper, 1961).

Bruner, Edward M., "Transformation of self in tourism," *Annals of Tourism Research*, Volume 18, Issue 2, 1991.

Casson, Lionel, *Travel in the Ancient World* (Allen & Unwin, 1974).

Chambers, Erve, *Tours Native: The Anthropology of Travel and Tourism* (Waveland Press, 2000).

Day, Matthew, "Auschwitz museum hit by thefts as visitors remove 'souvenirs' from Nazi death camp," *Telegraph Online*, May 5, 2014.

Downey, Dennis, and Raymond Hyser, *No Crooked Death: Coatesville Pennsylvania and the Lynching of Zachariah Walker* (University of Illinois Press, 1990).

Elton-Pym, James, "Calls for a crackdown on 'knockoff' Aboriginal souvenirs made in China and Bali," *National Indigenous Television* online, August 22, 2016.

Feifer, Maxine, *Tourism in History: From Imperial Rome to the Present* (Stein and Day, 1986).

Findlen, Paula, and Pamela Smith, eds., *Merchants and Marvels: Commerce, Science, and Art in Early Modern Europe* (Routledge, 2001).

Fussell, Paul, *The Norton Book of Travel* (W. W. Norton, 1987).

Gordon, Beverly, "The Souvenir: Messenger of the Extraordinary," *Journal of Popular Culture*, Winter 1986.

Gray, J. Glenn, *The Warriors: Reflections on Men in Battle* (Harper and Row, 1959).

Grescoe, Taras, *The End of Elsewhere: Travels Among the Tourists* (Serpent's Tail, 2004).

Hardt, Anton, *Adventuring Further in Souvenir Spoons* (Greenwich Press, 1971).

Harrington, John Walker, "Postal Carditis and Some Allied Manias," *American Magazine*, March 1906.

Howard, Donald R., *Writers and Pilgrims: Medieval Pilgrimage Narratives and Their Posterity* (University of California Press, 1980).

"Industry Profile: Gift, Novelty, and Souvenir Stores," *First Research*, April 17, 2017.

Lee, Hannah, "A Dialogue In Ivory: Thoughts on sixteenth century Afro-Portuguese salt cellars in the British Museum," *Unmaking Things*, Victoria and Albert Museum & Royal College of Art, 2013.

Levinson, Jerrold, ed., *The Oxford Handbook of Aesthetics* (Oxford University Press, 2003).

Lewis, Danny, "How Tourism Shaped Photography in 19th Century Japan," *Smithsonian*, October 28, 2015.

Löfgren, Orvar, *On Holiday: A History of Vacationing* (University of California Press, 1999).

Love, Lisa L., and Peter S. Sheldon, "Souvenirs: Messengers of Meaning," *Advances in Consumer Research*, Volume 25, 1998.

"Lynching in America: Confronting the Legacy of Racial Terror," *Equal Justice Initiative*, February 10, 2015.

MacCannell, Dean, *The Tourist: A New Theory of the Leisure Class* (University of California Press, 1976).

Macleod, Donald V. L., and James G. Carrier, eds., *Tourism, Power and Culture: Anthropological Insights* (Channel View Publications, 2010).

McPhee, John, "Travels of the Rock," *New Yorker*, February 26, 1990.

Potts, Rolf, "Cannibal Habits of the Common Tourist," *Los Angeles Review of Books*, November 15, 2013.

Rickly, Jillian, "Authenticity & Aura: A Benjaminian Approach to Tourism," *Annals of Tourism Research*, January 2012.

Rigby, Douglas, and Elizabeth Rigby, *Lock, Stock, and Barrel: The Story of Collecting* (J. B. Lippincott Company, 1944).

Roach, Mary, "Say Hello to My Little Friend," *Outside*, January 2012.

Robbins, Joel, and Holly Wardlow, eds., *The Making of Global and Local Modernities in Melanesia* (Routledge, 2005).

Schogol, Jeff, "U.S. Troops' war souvenirs are strictly regulated,"
     Stars and Stripes, April 11, 2006.

Schone, Mark, "Calvin Gibbs, Leader of 'Thrill Kill' Soldiers,
     Guilty of Murder," *ABC News* online, November 10, 2011.

Schouten, Frans, "The Process of Authenticating Souvenirs" from
     *Cultural Tourism in a Changing World: Politics, Participation
     and (Re)presentation*, Melanie K. Smith and Mike Robinson,
     eds. (Channel View Publications, 2006).

Silverberg, Michael, "Some 9/11 souvenirs that would be better
     than a cheese plate," *Quartz*, May 27, 2014.

Smith, Valene L., ed., *Hosts and Guests: The Anthropology of
     Tourism* (Blackwell, 1978).

Speake, Jennifer, ed., *Literature of Travel and Exploration: An
     Encyclopedia* (Routledge, 2003).

Stewart, Susan, *On Longing: Narratives of the Miniature, the
     Gigantic, the Souvenir, the Collection* (Duke University Press,
     1984).

Stutzenberger, Albert, *American Historical Spoons* (Charles E.
     Tuttle, 1971).

Sumption, Jonathan, *Pilgrimage* (Faber & Faber, 1975).

Swanson, Kristen K., "Souvenirs: Icons of meaning,
     commercialization and commoditization," *Tourism
     Management*, June 2012.

"The spectre of slavery haunts George Washington's house,"
     Economist, January 5, 2017.

Vincent, James, "Treasure trove of Apollo 11 souvenirs discovered
     in Neil Armstrong's home," *Verge*, February 10, 2015.

Walker, Rob, "Building Value," *New York Times Magazine*, May 21,
     2006.

Wang, Ning, "Rethinking Authenticity in Tourism Experience,"
     Annals of Tourism Research 26, no. 2 (1999): 349–70.

Weingartner, James J., "Trophies of War: U.S. Troops and the Mutilation of Japanese War Dead, 1941–1945," *Pacific Historical Review*, February 1992.

Witkowski, Terrence H., and Yoshito Yamamoto, "Omiyage Gift Purchasing By Japanese Travelers in the U.S.," *Advances in Consumer Research*, Volume 18, 1991.

Young, Harvey, "The Black Body as Souvenir in American Lynching," *Theatre Journal*, December 2005.

INDEX

Note: Page references for illustrations appear in *italics*.

197533